FINDING A VOICE

FINDING A VOICE

Communicating the Ecumenical Movement

Marlin VanElderen

William B. Eerdmans Publishing Company

Grand Rapids, Michigan / Cambridge, U.K.

© 2000 WCC Publications

This edition published 2001
by Wm. B. Eerdmans Publishing Co.

Wm. B. Eerdmans Publishing Co.
255 Jefferson Ave. S.E., Grand Rapids, Michigan 49503 /
P.O. Box 163, Cambridge CB3 9PU U.K.

Printed in the United States of America

05 04 03 02 01   5 4 3 2 1

ISBN 0-8028-4930-X

www.eerdmans.com

Contents

CONTENTS

CONTENTS

CONTENTS

Introduction

I vividly remember my first and only visit to Grand Rapids, Michigan. It was to entice Marlin VanElderen and his family to come to Geneva and join the WCC staff as the editor of *One World*. The dinner we shared was delicious, Meribeth's famous broccoli and chicken recipe, but the conversation was difficult. Marlin was a reluctant starter in the ecumenical marathon. Deeply immersed in his Christian Reformed heritage, his questions about the direction of the ecumenical movement were sharp and hard to answer then.

Two decades later, they still are, but not hard enough to prevent Marlin from establishing himself as a veteran ecumenist who has helped to shape the movement he came to love and give his life to, wholeheartedly.

This book is a tribute to his commitment and his skill as editor and writer, interpreting, remembering, sometimes chiding but always honouring the ecumenical cause.

He brought to that task an intellectual breadth and energy and a personal commitment and discipline that commanded the respect of everyone who came in contact with his work. Rigorously professional though his approach to editing was, you will still see glimpses in this collection of the man behind the keyboard. These are words coloured by his children's questions, the view from his window, the smell of coffee, the rhythm of the seasons and the echoes of half a hundred other voices.

In these brief essays, Marlin is tough and logical one minute as the relentless philosopher, irenic and wistful the next, and always eager to revel in the absurdity and contradiction of a movement whose rhetoric is always a step or three ahead of its reality. Between the lines you can hear his smile. Which is just as well because what he writes about is weighty, solemn stuff. He was the ever faithful chronicler of every meeting he attended, every decision made by the WCC.

Central committees, assemblies, annual overviews, endless reports and reviews — they were from early morning till late at night the bread and butter of Marlin's professional life. While many would have been swamped by the volume of the words, Marlin kept on reading, editing, rewriting, driven by a confidence that the Spirit is still speaking through the church and across the *oikoumene*.

He took the Council more seriously than many of its members, ever conscious of its role as a "privileged instrument" of the ecumenical movement. It was a privilege he took personally, trusting the Council's unique power to "set up signs", as the message from the Amsterdam assembly put it so precisely. Few of us could match Marlin's ability to discern and read those signs that give direction to the movement. And few could match his confidence that the movement would continue to surprise and delight us on our journey.

In his last editorial for *One World*, he talked about the problems inherent in the title of that late, great publication. He listed the risks of claiming too much and delivering too little, of sentimental universalism, of seeming to want to teach the world to sing the same song, Coca Cola style. Misconceptions the magazine faced, like the Council itself.

Marlin had addressed all those issues and a dozen more with unflinching honesty, but he ended by saying there was a more serious problem with *One World*, and that was that the magazine could never live up to the breathtaking catholicity suggested by its title.

That Marlin lived for so long and struggled so creatively and so faithfully with that problem is perhaps the best compliment we can pay him at his untimely death.

As I assembled the editorials that make up this book, still caught up in Marlin's loss, I had to wonder who would continue the work he did so well as an ecumenical editor. His death is a huge blow to the movement, leaving us as he did in mid-flight, robbed of time to stand back and reflect on those changes and chances of ecumenical life that can only be understood in hindsight.

We needed him to help us find out just why it is that the movement and its institutions are in such a state of crisis, and why ecumenical communication, once a proud vocation supported by budgets, structures, eager audiences and skilled practioners, now languishes in disarray.

But no sooner has that complaint settled on the page than a nagging doubt arises. Hasn't the ecumenical movement always been blessed and cursed by old ecumenists misreading change and new directions as decline and disarray? The "things ain't what they used to be" mentality has long thrived in ecumenical circles.

Marlin resisted this mindset. He somehow learned to live in a state of constant update, inside the whirlwind that is the ecumenical adventure and surviving the endless rearrangements that its institutions undergo. The cost of being so close to such turmoil is very high, but willingness to take that risk is one that faces all good ecumenical communicators.

What it amounts to is a commitment constantly to stand outside your comfort zone, in between the inherited certainties of creed and culture, to listen carefully to and sometimes absorb the cries of the angry and dispossessed, to learn to live with the contradiction of seeing people who have nothing compared to you in material terms, and yet are often richer and wiser about life and much clearer about God.

Ecumenism in our time can best be communicated from inside the eye of the storm. Its formulations will be messy, its boundaries fuzzy, and the ability of the churches to comprehend the changes will be as haphazard as ever.

Handling all that with grace makes for a demanding vocation. Marlin fulfilled that calling with distinction. His legacy inspires those of us left to carry on, and even more importantly, those who have yet to begin telling the story of the ecumenical movement.

If the man from Grand Rapids could do it, then so could we.

It is a job that waits to be done, more urgently now than ever before.

JOHN BLUCK
Dean of Christchurch Cathedral, New Zealand
Formerly WCC director of communications and editor of One World

FINDING A VOICE

Finding a voice. It's a helpful, if limited, figure of speech. It hints that the undertones and overtones which inevitably accompany our words determine how we'll be understood or misunderstood. It isn't just what we say, but our "tone of voice" which communicates. Not that the substance of what we say doesn't matter. Paul's caution to tongues-speaking Corinthians is a good reminder for writers and editors: "If you utter speech that is not intelligible, you will be speaking into the air" (1 Cor. 14:9).

Finding a voice. The words remind an editor (as if the task were not already daunting enough) that not only is his or her own voice one of many asking for a hearing, but also that this voice will doubtless have to change, particularly when undertaking a magazine that dares to call itself *One World*.

The point of changing one's voice, of course, is to be heard better. The "voice crying in the wilderness" is a vivid image, with good biblical credentials, but if nobody seems to be listening to us, that isn't by itself a guarantee of our faithfulness. This two-sided reality of the communications process is all too easy for an editor to lose sight of. The relentless pressure of deadlines obliges one to finish the next issue before most readers have received the last one.

Finding a voice. The image breaks down if it is seen as suggesting that finding *one* voice is possible or even desirable. A magazine is, after all, not a piece for solo voice, unaccompanied. Nor should it be an exercise in forcing pleasant harmonies out of discord.

The Bible reminds us that the dazzling and bewildering variety of human contexts calls for flexible speaking. The God who answered Moses in thunder at Mount Sinai (Exodus 19) passes by Elijah in the wind and earthquake and fire and speaks to him only in "a still, small voice" (1 Kings 19). For the writer of Proverbs, "Wisdom cries aloud in the streets" (1:20); from the prophet's point of view, the Spirit-filled servant does not "cry or lift up his voice or make it heard in the street" (Isaiah 42:2). And if some of Jesus' sayings perplexed most of his hearers then (and many since), there was little doubt about his meaning on many other occasions.

Finding a voice, then, may mean acknowledging that there are many voices. Sometimes they won't blend well. Especially this will happen when we take on the awesome task of giving a voice to the voiceless. The role of advocacy is an honourable one, but it is seldom an easy part to play. To use the power of speech which we take for granted to say a word on behalf of those who cannot speak can only mean interjecting hesitant and discordant notes.

But even if finding a voice is in the end too lofty an ideal to expect to achieve, the ongoing search is still worth the trouble. It's a search, though, that an editor cannot conduct without listening to the voice of the readers.

January/February 1983

SOJOURNERS

It was a short item on the 7 o'clock news, that five-minute dose of reality between sleep and the tasks of the day. A group of people in Switzerland, so it was reported, believe that the time has come to do something about what they see as the increasing dangers posed by refugees flooding into the country. Switzerland, they argue, is a small and crowded place; and there are limits to the population it can support. And when you have to start enforcing those limits, it's the Swiss people whose needs have to be given priority over the desires of foreigners.

Short items in a five-minute newscast may sometimes provide tempting grist for the mills of editorial-writers. But what struck me at 7:00 on that morning was a more personal reflection. I am not a refugee, but I am — like many of my colleagues at the World Council of Churches — a foreigner living in Switzerland. I can hold a paying job, rent a flat, send my children to school, own a car here only because I have an official form granting me permission to live and work in Geneva. And I have that official form only because I had the promise of a paying job in the first place.

Suppose (I thought as I got ready for work) a campaign to reduce the number of foreigners in Switzerland were to reach into the communications department of the WCC. More specifically, suppose the permission for *me* to live and work here were withdrawn. What would it be like for our family to try to reverse the process of adjusting ourselves to life in a foreign country? Where would we live? How would we support ourselves? Would the title of Thomas Wolfe's famous novel become some kind of haunting epithet for our life's story: *You Can't Go Home Again?*

It was about that point in my reflections when it suddenly dawned on me that this disquieting but utterly unlikely scenario was a heart-rending reality for throngs of Africans at that very moment, and a genuine daily fear for countless "undocumented aliens" elsewhere in the world. While I may be embarrassed by the thought that some Swiss shopkeeper, recognizing the lamentable accent and even more inadequate vocabulary which characterize my best efforts at speaking French, might resent me as an intruder, millions of other people are losing or stand to lose far more than their pride because of their status as aliens.

Such ramblings of the early-morning imagination hardly qualify as "identifying with the oppressed". But they do point, however feebly, to the need for those of us whose vulnerability to external forces is shielded by layers of social and economic and legal and ethnic protection to see beyond the statistics of human misery, as Methodist minister from New Zealand Charles Hailwood points out in the Bible study in this issue.

Who can comprehend the reality of hundreds of thousands of Ghanaians leaving Nigeria? Or the threat of expulsion facing millions of other foreigners without documents in the US, in South America, in Europe, in Australia, in the states of the Persian Gulf? The images on television or on the front page of the newspaper make some kind of impression, of course; but the TV crews move on to their next assignment and the newspaper will wrap tomorrow's garbage. Emergency appeals for material aid will draw generous contributions and relieve much suffering. Careful analysis of economic and political trends may help us "see this all in perspective".

The one whom we encounter in the gospels, the one who wept over the men and women and children of Jerusalem, would doubtless see more than a "human interest" story here, more than a mandate for sacrificial giving, more than an occasion for deepening our understanding of unjust social structures. Those homeless ones, forced to go home again, are, one by one, the image of his God — and ours.

March 1983

FREEZING OUT GOD

In addressing a group of American evangelicals not long ago, the President of the United States — so a *Washington Post* columnist tells us — "injected God into the debate over a nuclear freeze". For the *Post* writer Mr Reagan's language, which located a nuclear freeze on the negative side in the struggle between "right and wrong, good and evil", evoked memories of Elmer Gantry, the disreputable demagogic revival preacher of Sinclair Lewis's famous American novel.

Of course, many Christians not only dispute Mr Reagan's view that support for a nuclear freeze is tantamount to sin, but they take precisely the opposite position. Even so, any suggestion that it is demagoguery to construe this issue as one of "right and wrong, good and evil" is an ominous one.

On the nuclear freeze question, "the deity has been all over the lot", the *Post* writer chortles, "claimed by both proponents and opponents". He contends that there are enough "policy reasons, logical reasons, intellectual reasons" at stake in the freeze debate to make moral or religious arguments unnecessary.

It seems inevitable that, when churches seek to influence governments by offering moral and religious perspectives on a question, some political leaders will choose to respond in kind. Just because such a response may take on the aspects of "demagoguery", it doesn't follow that the issue is not a moral one.

Mr Reagan's use of theological categories in rejecting a nuclear freeze as sinful, however mistaken or regrettable other Christians may find it to be, is the price to be paid for having pointed out the moral issues in the debate in the first place. It no more removes this issue from the moral realm than, say, the white South African "biblical justification" of apartheid rules out moral discussion of that country's racial policies — though it surely doesn't make it any easier.

True, the writer may mean only to argue that Mr Reagan's approach to the nuclear freeze has misplaced the moral issue, confusing a strategy with its goal. But that argument could hardly be endorsed by those within the churches who call for a freeze on moral grounds. Besides, the very judgment that a question is or is not a "moral issue" has moral dimensions — as the protracted debate on abortion demonstrates. And the claim that it is possible to discuss the nuclear freeze without reference to moral issues hardly proves that one *ought* to do so.

Yet there is a salutary warning for Christians in what the *Post* columnist says. It is a summons to a modesty which begins by recognizing that the language of the church in public discussions will never quite fit. That may tempt us to alter that language fundamentally, so that it does fit: but as Helmut Thielicke warns, "when theology says only what the world can say to itself, it says nothing. The feet of those who will remove it are already at the door." Still, we must remember that many will be eager to argue that because moral language doesn't fit, or because those who use it don't always agree, the church should keep its opinions to itself.

April 1983

HEALING LAUGHTER

Let your acceptance change us
so that we may be moved
in living situations
to do the truth in love;
to practise your acceptance
until we know by heart
the table of forgiveness
and laughter's healing art.

I always feel a bit uneasy singing the last line of that stanza from Fred Kaan's* familiar ecumenical hymn (*Cantate Domino*, no. 137). I grew up thinking of laughter as vaguely irreverent: after all, no one ever laughed in church. Acceptance, doing the truth in love, forgiveness — those are Christian themes one can grasp, even if usually it is only in falling short that we see them. But "laughter's healing art"?

Most of what the churches are concerned about together or seek to do together seems either too bleak or too complex and delicate to provide a context for laughter. Much of what people laugh about in this world hinges on irony, but the irony of servitude in the 1980s on the very island where Toussaint L'Ouverture led a slave revolt in the 1790s is not the source of humour. Violence in Lebanon, murder in El Salvador, the church on trial in South Africa — the mere suggestion that laughter might be appropriate seems far more irreverent than even laughing in church used to. And if as the sadness of the situa-

---

* United Reformed Church in the United Kingdom, West Midlands Province moderator.

tions were not enough, the built-in difficulties the ecumenical movement faces in formulating a common opinion and drafting a common statement on public issues ensure that whatever is said is not going to sparkle with wit.

Of course, institutions can't laugh in any case. The danger is that when our exposure to the complexities and realities and inequalities and suffering of the world is mediated through institutions, as it usually must be, we may forget how to laugh. And if laughter is out of reach, what point is there in singing about its "healing art"?

Certainly not all — perhaps not even most — laughter is healing. Joyless laughter at the expense of those who are weeping over their own failures is little more than smug self-righteousness. Trivializing what others say or do may be a thin disguise for taking ourselves more seriously than we deserve to be taken. Humanity's first temptation — to be like God — may also overcome us when we comfortably assume that God, too, is mocking what we are making fun of.

Healing laughter demands grace and wisdom — as the hymn suggests by linking it with forgiveness and *practice*. Still, we do well to be uneasy about laughter's potential for healing, not least because it is impossible to take seriously. Yet in a suffering world and divided church, laughing together may — by God's grace — sometimes offer a glimpse of the healing for which we pray.

May 1983

THE COMPLEXITY OF UNITY

For a philosopher, it would seem, there are few concepts simpler than the idea of "oneness". There is something tidy, uncomplicated and irreducible about *one* — a simplicity that you lose when you move on to *several* or *many*.

But when you turn from the abstractions of philosophy to look at the concrete realities of the church, oneness suddenly becomes a very complex thing. Any reader of *One World* will recognize again and again that a painful paradox lurks in the magazine title. Perhaps it is the exclusive privilege of astronauts to see *one* world.

Our June issue is no exception to this general rule. The World Council of Churches faces its sixth assembly with a solid record of affirmations — in no uncertain terms — of the unity of the body of Christ. Every time we recite those words from the Nicene Creed — "we believe in *one* holy catholic and apostolic church" — we pronounce an implicit judgment on the status quo. Yet lying between the humbling acknowledgment that disunity in the church is unfaithful to our confession and disobedient to God and the realization of the oneness we confess, there are numerous steps, most of them difficult to take, some of them painful.

Paging through the articles that follow will expose some of the knotty elements that make unity among those who confess the name of Christ a far cry from the philosopher's simple oneness. Even when two denominations in a small country share a confessional heritage and a solid and growing record of working together, their eventual oneness is not a foregone conclusion, but an act of faith that requires an intricately planned process unfolding over a period of years. In another country Christian churches risk missing out on unprecedented

9

opportunities to help form a social consensus that takes gospel values into account — because they haven't had enough practice working together.

Dividing walls once built up between churches along lines of race may be rebuilt and extended along lines of how to deal with racism. Those concerned about the community of women and men in the church may sometimes even find the ideal of unity being used as an argument against doing justice.

Examples of such obstacles could easily be multiplied. Unity is something to be worked for and prayed for. Its compelling vision may grip some of us; but we can never take its motivating power for granted. There is too much evidence for describing the goal of unity in the same terms as G. K. Chesterton used for the ideal of Christianity: not that it has been tried and found wanting, but that too often it has been found difficult and not tried.

Another perhaps more subtle hazard confronts those who long for the unity of the church, who are eager to work and pray for it, but want to retain a firm grip on reality. It is the danger of discovering obstacles to unity everywhere else while forgetting that it is our own tendencies to fragment and divide for which we are responsible in the first instance.

Judgment must begin with the household of God, the apostle said (1 Peter 4:17). That strikes close to home. It's tempting to compile lists of barriers to unity in churches around the world. It's less appealing to look at how far we ourselves fall short of living up to our confession of the unity of the church. And although church unity is a complicated business, it probably won't be too difficult to recognize some causes for its absence even in ourselves.

June 1983

PART OF THE STORY

"What happened at the WCC's sixth assembly?" It's a difficult question to do justice to, but "What did it mean?" is probably an impossible one. In an important sense, answers to this question lie several years in the future. Certainly that is so from the point of view of the WCC as an institutional instrument of the ecumenical movement. Drawing even the broad lines of Vancouver's consequences for the Council's activities (for example, by way of the deliberations of the "core groups" appointed for each programme unit) is still several months away. And it will take much longer than that to fit these hints of the meaning of Vancouver into the larger picture of how the member churches are understanding and acting on their call and commitment to "unity, that the world might believe".

So, by the time "the meaning of the sixth assembly" is a subject on which cautious ecumenical observers and historians are willing to pronounce, it's safe to say that most of the detail described by journalists trying to tell what happened at Vancouver will be forgotten.

That realization — and the fact that a WCC assembly diverts a lot of money and time from other important activities — leads periodically to the suggestion that they be done away with. Asked about this at a press conference in Vancouver, WCC deputy general secretary Konrad Raiser admitted that assemblies are "problematic and in some ways ineffective". But, he added, "so far, assemblies are the only effective way we have found of assuring a sense of continuity and forward-looking in the ecumenical movement".

Such a forward look has less to do with specific planning for the WCC than with a maturing *vision* of unity among all Christians. Of course, to think of Vancouver in visionary terms can be dangerous. Vision too easily becomes a comforting haven for the escapist in all of us, the beginnings of a slide from faith into triumphalism.

The danger is real. In the glow of worshipping together with Christians of many countries and languages and confessional traditions on a sunny Sunday morning in Vancouver, realities were sometimes easy to forget: for all our theological convergence, doctrine still divides; for all the many languages in which we prayed and sang together, only five European ones were "official"; for all the fellowship we were about to enjoy at lunch in the cafeteria, the abundance of that meal is foreign to most of the world's people.

But if vision is hazardous, lack of vision is fatal. Peter's inept suggestion that he build some tents on the mountaintop so that the experience of Jesus' Transfiguration could last a while (Matthew 17:4) did not prove that those who dismiss the gospel as an illusion have it right. Missing the point is one thing; refusing to acknowledge that there is a point is quite another. And the danger of seeing only the high points of Vancouver's celebrative life together is probably less acute than the peril posed by the cynicism of those who would like to explain it all away.

To the extent to which Vancouver's meaning is determined by the vision it fostered, what happened there to those who were present is only part of the story. The whole story involves the whole people of God. And that's why the story of the sixth assembly is worth telling.

September 1983

BELIEVING WITHOUT SEEING

"When I was 17, it was a very good year." So began a popular ballad a few years ago. The singer looked nostalgically back to particular times in his life and compared those years with vintage wines.

Not many of us would be inclined to call 1983 "a very good year". One hardly needs to be reminded of the reasons for passing such a negative judgment on it. When the media release their lists of the "top ten news stories of 1983", there will be no surprises, only unhappy and uneasy recollections.

Many people will remember 1983 for events or trends that have touched them far more directly and immediately than the spectacular items the journalists list. For some it's a slow-moving catastrophe, like drought; for others a disaster that has been upstaged by a worse one elsewhere; for many it's the chronic oppression or poverty of a situation which has not changed for so long that it isn't "news"-worthy anymore.

Against the gloom of year-end assessments of the state of the world, a line from Swiss Reformed pastor Hans-Ruedi Weber is particularly striking.

The context is a prophecy of the coming Messiah, uttered during those gloomy years between Malachi and Matthew: "He . . . shall remove all darkness from under heaven, and there shall be peace in all the earth; . . . the earth shall be glad, and the clouds shall rejoice. . . ." Expectations like that were taken up with God's incarnation in Jesus, Weber writes. After the death of those who were eyewitnesses of God's mighty act in Jesus Christ, "the fulfilment of these expectations in Christ is only perceptible to those who believe without seeing."

What we often see — and are tempted to believe — are the forces

13

of death. For some Christians, those forces appear on a television screen or in the headlines of a newspaper. For many others, being "acquainted with grief" is a daily, first-hand reality, which they not only see but touch and taste. On the edge of a year that has, through George Orwell's famous novel *1984*, become a symbol of the frightening mess humanity is capable of making for itself, the call to believe without seeing might seem more like a counsel of despair than a word of hope.

But believing without seeing is not the same as wandering in darkness. The Christmas gospel that God is actively committed to the world and to humankind — recorded in scripture and woven through the history of the community of those who have through the centuries believed without seeing — is an ongoing story.

Some people are living by that kind of faith. Their stories unfold in places that may seem as out-of-the-way today as Bethlehem and Galilee did 2000 years ago — places like Lenasia, São Miguel Paulist, Gioiosa Ionica, Ebeye.

You probably won't find those names in the datelines of the major news stories of 1983 — not even in the lists compiled by religious journalists, whose eyes will naturally fall on events like a WCC assembly, an international congress of evangelists, a papal visit or a synod of Roman Catholic bishops. Nor are the stories here the kind that immediately elicit the nostalgic judgment that "it was a very good year". But neither fame nor nostalgia is particularly helpful for those who are struggling to believe without seeing.

December 1983

THE THING WITH FEATHERS

The poet Emily Dickinson once described hope as "the thing with feathers/That perches in the soul,/And sings the tune without the words,/And never stops at all."

Looking around, we may be more inclined to observe that if hope is in fact like a bird, it's not because it sings within us, but because it tends to fly away at the slightest disturbance. Often it's not even a matter of *losing* hope: except for short-term things like the weather ("I hope it stops raining by the weekend"), hope is something we rarely have in the first place.

Against such a background of doubt, cynicism, even bitterness, the choice of "In Christ — Hope for the World" as the theme for the seventh assembly of the Lutheran World Federation is a courageous one. The affirmation is, of course, solidly biblical; but those who are accustomed to holding the Bible in one hand and the newspaper in the other will likely be very cautious when talking about hope and even more so when affirming it.

There are many other stories about the reality of Christian hope. The picture that emerges is a warning against the sort of hope that is a carefree or comfortable assumption that everything's going to turn out all right. For a church leader from China, hope for the growth and development of Christianity in his country is an ecumenical challenge. Bishop K. H. Ting, leader of the China Christian Council and the Three-Self Movement, came to Geneva hoping for the beginning of a dialogue that would be quite different from the way Western Christianity has often related to the Chinese church.

For Lutherans in Finland and Orthodox in the USSR, the hope of bridging centuries of mistrust and ignorance has taken shape in formal theological dialogues — hardly spectacular stuff, some might think, but nevertheless bearing fruit. Hope must sometimes learn to sustain itself with such small signs: consider, for example, the clergy training centres in Ethiopia, an indicator of the church's involvement in the vast development challenges in that country. And hope can, of course, be easily disappointed, as some young people in Australia's Uniting Church learned when their initiative for renewal of the church met with sharply critical responses in some quarters.

The future orientation of hope, its focus on what has not yet come to be, lies behind some memorable words of Reinhold Niebuhr: "Nothing that is worth doing can be achieved in our lifetime; therefore we must be saved by hope." Niebuhr then went on to add: "Nothing which is true or beautiful or good makes complete sense in any immediate context of history; therefore we must be saved by faith. Nothing we do, however virtuous, can be accomplished alone; therefore we are saved by love. No virtuous act is quite as virtuous from the standpoint of friend or foe as it is from our standpoint. Therefore we must be saved by the final form of love, which is forgiveness."

In a world that tends to scare away any singing in the soul, the "tune without the words" is not enough to make hope much more than a "thing with feathers", whistling past the graveyard. What we must learn and accept and learn again and again is that the good news of Christian hopes is never undemanding and seldom spectacular.

January/February 1984

ALL WE ARE SAYING . . .

"All we are saying is 'Give peace a chance'." Events of the 1980s have given new life to that protest song from the 1960s.

In a world where the logic of overkill prevails, there is much to be said in favour of such sanity and simplicity. These are words that voice the hopes for peace and anxieties about war felt by the children of the world. "Give peace a chance" is an impassioned yet thoroughly reasonable cry of outrage over astronomical arms expenditures, militarism and "peacekeeping" through making war. It can be an appeal for genuine realism, refusing to concede to the powerful the argument that "they" *must* know more than we do.

"Give peace a chance" can express the biblical vision of beating swords into ploughshares, the courage, in the face of a "balance of terror", to say (as the WCC's sixth assembly put it): "Fear not, for Christ has overcome the forces of evil."

Certainly slogans can be misleading, even dangerous. Catchy formulas can overlook or short-circuit the ambiguities and nuances of situations. Reduced to slogans, the deepest truths of the Christian faith can become worse than trivial. "A lot of the problem in Northern Ireland", warns Columbanus Community of Reconciliation member Annette Eisenmann, "has to do with vocabulary and phrases like 'are you saved?'"

To preface the words "Give peace a chance" with the claim that this is "all we are saying" does indeed risk turning a profound simplicity into an oversimplified slogan. For many people — if not most — "give peace a chance" is not *all* they are saying; and to pretend that it is may cloud important issues.

On the other hand, exegeting too closely the words of a song sung

17

at a peace demonstration may obscure the point that there are shared commitments beyond the affirmations we make separately — and that "give peace a chance" is one of those urgent and transcending appeals we ought not to issue alone.

For the churches in the ecumenical movement this question of what we say together is a perennial one. It is an issue which will be getting close attention in the WCC study "Towards the Common Expression of the Apostolic Faith Today". What the Faith and Order Commission is undertaking here is a complex historical and theological investigation to be sure; but everyday issues of Christian witness — not least the question of peace — are woven into it.

"When *I* use a word, it means just what I choose it to mean — neither more nor less." Sceptics will be quick to cite that remark of Humpty Dumpty to Alice (in Lewis Carroll's classic *Through the Looking Glass*) as proof of the impossibility of the task facing those seeking a common expression of the apostolic faith. Shelf after shelf of thick volumes in theological libraries seem to add their own weight of evidence for that kind of doubt. Accepting the same words does not always mean sharing the same beliefs. If "all we are saying" is the Nicene Creed, we still have a long way to go.

Undertaking the common expression of the apostolic faith can be a high-priced form of ecumenism. Daring to admit the presence of real differences — both when we use the same words and when we don't — will be a hazardous undertaking, calling for equal measures of faith and humility. The months and years ahead will show how far the churches are willing to give it a chance.

March 1984

EXPLAINING OURSELVES

Shortly before 8:00 one morning during the WCC's sixth assembly in Vancouver, Canada, I arrived in one of the communications offices with a trayful of breakfast, some of which I hoped to have time to eat before the nonstop activities of the day began. One bite into a piece of toast, and the telephone rang. At the other end of the line was an obviously agitated caller who wanted to speak to "somebody from the WCC".

"You people are guests here," she told me, "and you're being treated very well. What right do you have to criticize the government of this province? What do you know about British Columbia anyway?"

Not a great deal, I was obliged to admit, beyond a sort of rudimentary notion of the geography of the university campus which had been, physically speaking, my whole world for a week or so.

As the conversation continued, it became evident that what had aroused my caller's wrath was having heard through the local news media that some Canadian church leaders had spoken out against cuts in social programmes by the provincial government. Some of those critics were in Vancouver for the assembly, and what they were saying had been juxtaposed with or included in some news reporting of assembly events. An evaluation of the policies of the British Columbia government was not on the agenda of the assembly itself.

I don't know if I succeeded in making this distinction clear. But for me on that Vancouver morning the call was a particularly vivid reminder of the difficulty one faces when trying to tell the story of the World Council of Churches to people in whose consciousness the WCC is not an everyday reality.

It's as if the old parable of the blind men and the elephant — each

19

with a partial and thus utterly mistaken notion of what the beast is like, based on the limited part they have touched — were further complicated by some of the people touching something other than the elephant.

The problem is not of course restricted to organizations as broad and complex and diverse as the WCC. If there is a denominational headquarters anywhere in the world that has ever been criticized for being overly transparent to "the people in the pews", its story has yet to be told.

And even in most local congregations, the members who have what fulltime staff would consider an intimate awareness of the congregation's life are often a small minority. A minister friend of mine who had left the pastorate for a while once confessed to me his initial shock upon learning how seldom a group of business colleagues — all of whom he (correctly I think) considered "active lay people" — discussed *church* matters over lunch. His point was not to question their sincerity or commitment, but to admit his own clerical tunnel vision.

"Know yourself" was Socrates' famous dictum. In a climate of criticism of the ecumenical movement, one is tempted to describe the challenge of communicating the ecumenical vision as succinctly: "Explain yourself". Both mandates are easily stated and fearfully difficult to follow.

But ecumenical explaining is a process that must work in both directions — and not always as neatly as one might like. No one has a monopoly on "the answers". The notion that one has — or ought to have — the answers can itself be a dangerous delusion.

April 1984

PILGRIMS WITH ROOTS

Pitching a large tent for participants in the WCC's sixth assembly to gather in for worship began as a necessity: finding a place for 4,000 people to worship together. The excitement of what went on in the tent transformed a necessity into a virtue. Subsequent reflection has elevated the tent to a symbol.

Like the biblical tabernacle, the Vancouver tent expresses the pilgrim aspect of the church in this world, ready to pull up stakes in response to human need, disdaining the glorious permanence of lavish structures because of the immobility they almost inevitably foster.

The Bible is a rich source for pilgrim imagery. Many such stories are summed up in Hebrews 11, which describes a succession of heroes of faith as people who "acknowledged that they were strangers and exiles on the earth . . . seeking a homeland. They desired a better country, that is, a heavenly one."

But like all images, the picture of a pilgrim church can be one-sided. A much-needed warning against the church's temptation to power politics and empire-building can be misinterpreted when mobility and flexibility are glamourized (particularly by those for whom the "pilgrim church" is a figure of speech which causes them no personal vulnerability). For people also look to the church for the spiritual sustenance and consolation of the gospel. Its vocation is not only to afflict the comfortable, but to comfort the afflicted.

The story of South Africa's uprooted townships shows some of the dilemmas that this dual vocation can cause for the pilgrim church. Its subject is people for whom "moving" is perhaps too bitter an experience to serve as a metaphor for the church on the move. And the effects of forced removals in South Africa are devastating, not least of them being loss of contact with the church.

How does the church respond to the needs of those uprooted people? If it seeks with the means at its disposal to alleviate the conditions of misery in which they are forced to live, will this have the effect of diverting attention from a fundamental injustice? Will this tend to take the heat off a government that tramples on the rights of its citizens and calls them aliens in their own country?

Such questions are not uniquely posed by the South African situation, of course. All over the world the pilgrim church, having followed the victims into the wilderness, faces the question of what to do next.

It's a dilemma for which there are no ready-made formulas. The pilgrim church may be so well travelled that it overemphasizes the "breadth and length" of the love of Christ to the exclusion of the "height and depth". Perhaps it takes a mixed metaphor to describe the challenge to God's people: how can you be on the move while growing out of deep roots and building on firm foundations?

May 1984

PRECISELY . . .

All but a few people agree that our planet more nearly resembles, say, a basketball than a basketball court. This eliminates the fear of falling over the edge, but it creates a challenge for map-makers, who are commonly obliged to present their work on flat sheets of paper. What they draw is inevitably a distorted picture of the spaces they depict.

In 1974 the German cartographer Arno Peters produced a map which is said to represent all the land masses on the earth's surface accurately in terms of their area. To do so, he had to portray continents and islands with somewhat different shapes from those on the familiar Mercator projection map, which dates from the 16th century and allots two-thirds of its space to the Northern Hemisphere.

According to *Religious News Service,* a controversy has arisen over the Peters projection. The newsletter of the Institute for Religion and Democracy, a US organization often critical of what it sees as pro-third-world bias in the ecumenical movement, recently called it a "presentation of the world in ideological fashion". Church groups and United Nations agencies, by contrast, hail the Peters map as correcting the northern bias of other maps. Says Ward Kaiser of Friendship Press in New York, which is distributing the map: "We see this map as being very central to the establishment of a correct worldview."

A curious objection to emerge in this fray comes from the author of a standard textbook on map-making. He complains that the Peters map has "all the angles . . . wrong for navigating". Now surely few if any of those intrepid sailors and balloonists who periodically tackle the ocean alone in fragile crafts would steer by a Peters projection map. So the critique of its distortion of shapes and thus of directions need not cause too much alarm. But the objection is an interesting reflection of the evident obsession our era has with a certain kind of accuracy.

Technology has made it possible to satisfy this craving for precision in ways our ancestors — probably to their credit — never dreamed of. The proliferation of digital quartz watches, for instance, enables just about anyone to answer the question "What time is it?" with an accuracy formerly reserved to organizations like the Royal Observatory in Greenwich. (Never mind that it takes most of us longer to grasp "11:48 and 52 seconds" than "About ten minutes to twelve".)

Ron O'Grady, vice-chairman of the Asian Christian Art Association, observes that, had theologians listened to the testimony of Asian Christian artists at a recent conference in Manila, "an angry debate about syncretism and dialogue" would no doubt have started. This suggests a check on our eagerness for a certain sort of precision. Compared with theologians, O'Grady says, visual artists "have another kind of wisdom". So, we might add, do rural women and poets and children and even, perhaps, journalists.

Now many people understand that the theologian's job is precisely to be precise, whether describing the procession of the Holy Spirit, the mode of Christ's presence in the eucharist or interfaith dialogue. Church history is rife with heresy trials showing how difficult that is within a single confessional context. And fifty years of Faith and Order work on Baptism, Eucharist and Ministry testify to the complexities of doing theology precisely in an ecumenical setting.

The point is not to malign theological precision. Rather, the question is: does the laborious quest for precisely stated positions on ecumenical issues close our thinking to insights from others and polarize our discussions around our own finely honed views?

June 1984

GREAT EXPECTATIONS?

Journalist Garry Wills once wrote a scathing critique of how his media colleagues dealt with Pope John Paul II's 1979 visit to the US.

Largely ignorant of religious issues, the press (so Wills charged) suspended their critical faculties and focused only on the visit's human interest, trivial and entertainment elements, obscuring substantive and intriguing questions it might have provoked. Well-regarded weekly columnists, usually reputed to be more reflective than those pressed by deadlines to write news stories for tomorrow's front page, were no exception. And so readers got no real idea of what the pope's visit *meant*.

Maybe Wills overstated the case. Anyway, I've come to feel a certain sympathy for those who try to explain the meaning of a papal visit after Pope John Paul II spent three hours at the WCC headquarters. Interpreting that event, painstakingly arranged ahead of time, would be easier if it had produced clear and immediate and specifiable results which one could itemize as "the meaning of the pope's visit". A little reflection shows why it didn't.

For one thing, relations between the Roman Catholic Church and the WCC and its 301 [now 337] member churches of more than a dozen traditions are extremely complex. Certainly both are committed to participation together in "the one ecumenical movement"; but there are obvious differences between a council of churches and a church with "a world-wide extension".

Furthermore, behind the last two decades of closer contacts and collaboration loom centuries of separation, mistrust and worse. So whether or not the papal visit was an ecumenical milestone won't be clear except in retrospect, years from now.

During the visit, while waiting for the closed session between Vatican and WCC representatives to end, I heard several people remark that the worship service which had preceded the private meeting had not been as exciting or dramatic as they had hoped.

Struck by the contrast between the reaction and the Wills critique of the hoopla surrounding the US papal visit, I was reminded of a New Testament story (Matthew 11) about a first-century "media event", the appearance of John the Baptist in the Judean wilderness. Here was a phenomenon whose "meaning" eluded even its main character — particularly when John found himself on Herod's Death Row. So he sends some followers to ask Jesus, "Are you in fact the One who was going to come?"

After reassuring them, Jesus turns to his own followers. "When you went out to John in the desert, *what did you expect to see?*" He then suggests that those lured by the spectacle of John's preaching into anticipating quick solutions and easy explanations didn't understand how that proclamation fitted into the history of God's saving activity.

The parallel between Matthew's account and our papal visit obviously breaks down at many points. Still, before we ask what the pope's visit to the WCC meant, it might be useful to come to clarity about the question "What did you expect to see?"

More important than whether expectations of vivid television images, spellbinding oratory or a dramatic ecumenical leap forward were realized is how this event fits into the ecumenical pilgrimage. That's an open-ended question, whose answer could not be predetermined by the visit.

The joint statement of the visit expresses some fairly specific challenges and commitments. These call Christians around the world to creative and persistent fleshing out of the encounter in Geneva. In many places this will be a matter of continuing and deepening existing ecumenical engagements that are sometimes, alas, undertaken with little if any official support.

July 1984

COVER STORY

People's faces are a fairly common subject for magazine covers. In fact, if you glance at the latest offerings on the news-stand, you'll frequently see the same face smiling or scowling from the covers of several current periodicals — whether it's an aspiring or recently elected political leader, a rock music superstar, an Olympic gold-medalist or the lead actor in a newly released film.

In the centre of the cover of this month's issue of *One World* there is a face without a name. It illustrates an article about how churches are responding to the devastating consequences of ongoing drought in Africa, so it may not even occur to us to wonder about the name that goes with the person shown there. And when we go on to read that according to some estimates six million people are in danger of death from starvation in Ethiopia alone, the thought that each of them has a face and a name only makes the statistic more unreal, more difficult for us to cope with.

How do we recognize Jesus in the faces of those whose names we don't know and never will know? How can we be expected to recognize Jesus in those millions more whose faces we'll never see in person or in photographs? Yet it's not easy to escape the impression that this is part of what Jesus meant when he made that uncomfortably close linkage between our response to him and our feeding the hungry, clothing the naked, visiting the sick and the imprisoned.

This is not just a call for compassion. That, of course, is part of the story. And perhaps pictures of faces — with or without names — do help to call forth or develop such human fellow-feeling. But, as pastor Emanuel Elouti of the Federation of Churches and Evangelical Missions of Cameroon points out, if you're talking about the drought in

Africa, compassion alone isn't going to begin to make a dent in the problem.

Of course, the magnitude of the problems and the dangers inherent in trying to confront them makes it very tempting to stop at compassion. "The crunch comes," says Christian Aid's former Africa area secretary Bridget Walker, "where there is pressure on people's lives." She was talking specifically about churches in Britain, but the point is easily enough applied everywhere else. When the problems hit close to our homes, we're more than ready to have the churches move beyond pity to a more significant involvement.

But to see Jesus in the face of the stranger — even when we don't see those faces — requires us to extend that vision beyond our own little circle. That's the ecumenical challenge.

October 1984

A LOT TO LEARN

Not long ago I came across a cartoon in a German magazine. The drawing depicted a totem pole in front of the headquarters of the WCC, casting a shadow on the building in the shape of a cross. Two people were standing next to the pole. One was obviously perplexed. The other was glibly explaining: "Well, you have to see these things in the right light."

It's meant ironically, of course. The one figure is probably supposed to be "the average churchgoer", puzzled to discover a totem pole on the grounds of the World Council of Churches. The jaunty explanation given by the other, clearly meant to represent an ecclesiastical bureaucrat, is a caricature of interfaith dialogue, which the editors of this periodical apparently regard as a blurring of the lines between Christianity and other religions.

Without a doubt, it's a clever drawing. By a few words and a few deft strokes of the pen, the cartoonist has given lively expression to a particular point of view about the totem pole presented to the Council during the sixth assembly in Vancouver in 1983 and about the broader issue of how Christians relate to persons of other faiths.

It's clever. Unfortunately, it's based on two serious misunderstandings. Not only does the drawing wrongly suggest that a totem pole is a pagan object of worship. It also implies that the interfaith dialogue in which the ecumenical movement is involved aims at a kind of crude syncretism, jumbling all religions together.

Not to be forgotten in any talk about the "meaning" of this totem pole is its impressive reality as a *gift* to the WCC from the Native peoples of Canada. And another prominent element in this pole's meaning is that it might become an occasion for "ecumenical education".

That suggests several possibilities — none of them uncomplicated. One area of learning is certainly a deeper recognition of the situation of Indigenous peoples all over the world and in Canada in particular — and the churches' responsibility for and in those situations. Another kind of ecumenical learning spurred by the presence of the totem pole is struggling together with the "dialogue of cultures" that is so central to the ecumenical movement. A deepened understanding of that encounter was a major concern to emerge from the sixth assembly.

"Given on the one hand the richness and variety of cultures, and on the other the conflict between the life-affirming and life-denying aspects within each culture," the assembly said, "we need to look again at the whole issue of Christ and culture in the present historical situation".

True ecumenical learning around the totem pole would be the exact opposite of the cartoonist's snide version of syncretistic shadow play. But if such genuine learning has nothing to do with baptizing the pole as a Christian symbol, neither will it trivialize the pole into a mere piece of fascinating folklore, a museum display to be visited, stared up at, photographed and forgotten until the returning tourists pass around their pictures of Switzerland.

And that, it's safe to say, is a lot to learn.

November 1984

CHRISTMAS STORIES

In the New Testament, angels play a fairly minor role. And they have attracted relatively little attention from Christian theology. Yet angels feature prominently in the gospel narratives of Jesus' birth.

Since the time the New Testament was written, centuries of Christian art and Christmas carols have given these heavenly heralds of the incarnation more than what might seem to be, from a purely theological point of view, their due. Among those familiar Bible verses that "everybody knows" are the words which the gospel of Luke puts in the mouth of angels: "Glory to God in the highest, and on earth peace among men in whom he is pleased".

An angel may be a suitable if extraordinary visual reminder that the birth celebrated at this season of the year was no ordinary event. But the fact that no angels appear in any of this month's *One World* articles points to a danger in our cover* as well. Maybe because few if any of us have direct experience with them, we can too easily fit angels into a romanticized version of the event Christmas commemorates.

In his book *On Being a Christian* Hans Küng warns against trivializing the celebration of Jesus' birth, "as if the 'holy infant so tender and mild' . . . were always smiling and had never cried in his very human misery. . . . As if the Saviour of the needy, born in a stable, had not clearly revealed a partisanship for the nameless ones (shepherds) against the great ones who are named (Augustus, Quirinius). As if the Magnificat of the grace-endowed maid, about the humiliation of the mighty and the exaltation of the humble, about satisfying the hungry

* A representation of an angel above the door of a church in Kotna, Papua New Guinea.

31

and sending away the rich, were not a militant announcement of a re-vision of priorities. As if the lovely night of the newborn child meant that we could ignore his work and his fate three decades later. . . .

"It is in fact obvious," Küng concludes, "that even the apparently idyllic Christmas story has very real social-critical implications and consequences."

During the dark days of the Vietnam war, the question arose every December of whether or not there would be a "Christmas truce" that year, and, if so, how faithfully it would be observed. (It didn't take too highly developed a sense of irony to recognize that the very idea of such a "truce" stood in profound judgment of the entire war.)

In a world where hatred festers and seethes in the town of Jesus' birth, in a world of hunger and disease and despair, in a world where massive resources of misspent energy go into propping up systems of injustice and oppression, in a world where even the ecumenically best intentioned of Christians must go their separate ways to the Lord's ta-ble, there is a strong temptation to take a sort of "Christmas truce" from being bombarded by such realities.

Such a breather is not an option for Palestinians in a refugee camp in Bethlehem or for children starving in Ethiopia or for blacks being uprooted from their homes in South Africa. And the rest of us cannot really understand the meaning of what the angels said about joy and peace and God's glory unless we refuse to treat the Christmas story as a mere inspiring legend which can be pulled out of the context of what its central figure said and did.

Accepting the Christmas message means accepting the implica-tions of confessing that the one whose birth was announced by angels still lives.

December 1984

BIBLE AND NEWSPAPER

Former Christian Conference of Asia staff member Harvey Perkins observes that Bible study must "be set in the world of human events and seek to discern God's will in the midst of them".

In the words of a familiar slogan, he says, Bible study as an ecumenical exercise requires "the Bible in one hand and the newspaper in the other".

That's a much-needed warning against two ways of treating the Bible — neither unfamiliar in the church — which have little in common except a tendency to insulate the Bible and life from each other.

One is the hijacking of the Bible by the sort of critical scholarship which leaves the impression that no one can really understand scripture without a thorough grounding in ancient history, ancient languages and a variety of other academic disciplines.

The Bible is an ancient book, written by many different people over the course of many centuries. It passed through various stages of transmission before achieving its present form. So what's needed for understanding the Bible on this view is a scholarly élite to analyze and penetrate through all of this historical and literary crust.

It takes neither a cynic nor an anti-intellectual to observe that the results of all this scholarly endeavour are sometimes contradictory and often more confusing than illuminating. That doesn't disallow biblical scholarship, of course, but it does suggest a certain measure of caution about some of its claims, particularly when it begins to sound as if the Bible can't speak to the contemporary world and our lives because we can't be sure of what it's saying.

Others, in Swiss Reformed pastor Hans-Ruedi Weber's words, see the Bible as a quarry from which prooftexts can be mined. Such a view goes to the opposite extreme. Instead of losing the text while exploring the labyrinths of its context, prooftexters ignore the context altogether.

They blithely quote a snatch of a sentence here, paraphrase part of a parable there, trot out a half-remembered story somewhere else — all in the interest of documenting what they already thought. The Bible may seem to be speaking to everyday life — but it is speaking in sentence fragments.

When a public figure like the president of the United States does that — in the interest of defending his policies in front of a Christian audience — editorialists rise up in alarm, rightly repudiating the implications that scripture is a kind of nose that can be twisted to any shape one likes.

But such misuse of the Bible surely transcends political preferences. There is little to choose between a needlepointed wall plaque which treats a biblical phrase like a magic talisman and a litter of little-thought-through parenthetical scripture references in the most imposing ecclesiastical document.

"The Bible in one hand and the newspaper in the other." It's a challenging concept, but this, too, calls for caution. For a great deal depends on *which* newspaper it is we have in our other hand.

That's one of the values of reading the Bible together ecumenically: the mutual correction which can happen when Christians who are reading different newspapers (and, far more importantly, operating from a background of different experiences) help each other to spot their misreadings.

May 1985

"WEEP FOR YOURSELVES . . ."

A US journalist researching an article on people's memories of the Vietnam War a decade later recently asked a Sunday school class of 17- and 18-year-old students if they could identify any of the following names: Ho Chi Minh, McNamara, the Chicago Seven, Thieu, Ky. None could.

His experience, commented *New Yorker* magazine, confirmed what others have observed. Young people with access to instant information in our "global village" tend to have a very low level of awareness of even recent events. "What the news has gained in volume and speed it appears to have lost in durability."

The magazine suggested that this may be related to the nature of the electronic media — which "offer the news in a present that has neither a past nor a future. . . . The pictures flicker on the screen and then are gone forever."

Perhaps. But my temptation to shake my head over the ignorance of the next generation was soon corrected. I can hardly flatter myself as a victim to the failings of youth anymore. And I spend a fair amount of time reading the news and very little watching it on television. Yet it dawned on me that I've long since lost track of the warring factions in Lebanon and I don't know why Iran and Iraq are still at war.

Gaps in one's knowledge of current events are of course embarrassing for an editor. But far worse is the loss of human feeling, the ease with which we accustom ourselves to the pain and suffering of others when we have no context to put it in.

In a poem with the chilling title "A Refusal to Mourn the Death, by Fire, of a Child in London", Dylan Thomas wrote: ". . . I shall not murder/The mankind of her going with a grave truth/Nor blaspheme

35

down the stations of her breath/With any further/Elegy of innocence and youth . . ./After the first death, there is no other."

The bleak hopelessness of the poet's claim that it dishonours the victims of unexplainable tragedies to use them as occasions for philosophizing may trouble us. How much more troubling our own far less thoughtful refusals to mourn the deaths of children and adults all over the world, by car bombs or sniper fire or hunger or a hundred other terrors!

Our eyes are dry because we've forgotten or never understood or dismissed from our overloaded minds the events and struggles and tangles of injustice that might explain the *how* of these deaths even if the *why* remains elusive.

Perhaps before reflecting about what the churches of the world can do ecumenically in the Middle East we need to listen more carefully to what the churches in the Middle East are sharing with the rest of us. Recall, for example, the eloquent experience of faith to which Lebanese Christian Frieda Haddad testified at the WCC's sixth assembly in Vancouver.

She spoke of a 1983 Easter service in war-ravaged Beirut as "the experience of death in the midst of life. A whole nation living under the sign of the cross, a country living under death, living in this constant boundary situation between death and life, reaching out with Thomas and feeling the sting of death in an immediate firsthand touch of the Risen Christ, and thus tasting the sweetness and glory of life confronting and overcoming death. . . .

"As you go through the purifying fire of boundary-situations all that is non-essential in you disappears. . . . To have experienced this over the last eight years is our way."

For many of us, weighted down by non-essentials, that isn't our way. To us, as to those who mourned Jesus on the way to the cross, come his words: "Weep for yourselves. . . ."

June 1985

THE UGLY TRUTH

Before writing this one Wednesday evening, I decided to watch at least a few minutes of a televised football match — the European football cup final in Brussels between Liverpool and Juventus of Turin.

The match in the end was irrelevant — a passionless charade enacted only to prevent a rekindling of the violence that had taken more than three dozen lives, injured hundreds of others and shocked millions of TV viewers around the world.

Despite the irony implicit in trying to answer "Why?" in cases of "senseless violence", hundreds of editorials have made the effort since that awful evening at Heysel stadium. Shock and outrage have gradually given way to attempted explanations.

Some are repeated over and over. Chronic unemployment, which leaves young people with the sense of having "no future", is near the top of everyone's list. Drunkenness. Poor organization — lax security outside the stadium and insufficient police protection and physical barriers inside — is also frequently cited.

Other suggestions are more debatable. People who would normally blush at ethnic stereotyping wonder aloud if football violence expresses a peculiarly English character flaw. Others blame Mrs Thatcher's dismantling of the welfare state. A Soviet commentator cast even more widely to catch the entire West in his explanatory net, though in subsuming the events in Brussels under the East-West conflict, he described football attendance in the USSR, by contrast, as something like theatre-going — a claim for which the evidence is apparently less than convincing.

Some point out that "organized hooliganism" lends a perverse sort of meaning to alienated people; and one hears that it was not football fans at all but neo-Nazis who started the trouble. A number of commentators argue that ineffective governance and lax officiating have made football itself a model of violence, though one editorial I read went further to locate the problem in the very fact of "competition", which pervades society today.

Apart from the sociological and psychological explanations and speculations, I was reminded while reflecting on the Brussels tragedy of what the second letter to the Thessalonians calls "the mystery of lawlessness . . . already at work" (2:7).

The point of this goes deeper than glib fashionable professions of collective guilt ("We are all assassins", concluded one editorial, though the writer was clearly not proposing to turn himself in at the nearest police post). The sobering reality is that the evil which happened at Heysel stadium was far more than the sum of the individual misdeeds of those who threw bricks or charged through grandstands swinging makeshift clubs.

To be sure, most of us — to the extent that we talk about evil at all — are probably more at home with theoretical and impersonal discussions of "structures" and "systems" that with the apostle's apocalyptic vocabulary of "the rebellion", "the son of perdition", "the restrainer" and the ultimate slaying of "the lawless one" by the breath of the Lord Jesus' mouth.

But watching the horror of Heysel unfold was a useful reminder that underneath our detached and analytical theories lies the ugliness of sin — and its inexplicability. In the face of such graphic displays of the "mystery of lawlessness", it takes a lot of faith to look for visible evidence of the mystery of grace.

One thing seems certain from what the New Testament tells us: the signs of the kingdom won't be as spectacular and obvious as what we saw on television from a stadium called Heysel.

July 1985

NOT FOR EXPERTS ONLY

"Are you reading something interesting?" a colleague asked as he walked into my office.

I held up a copy of the report, "The International Financial System: An Ecumenical Critique". "Have you seen it?"

"No thanks," he said with a grin. "I think I'll pass that one by!"

My friend's reaction was hardly surprising or untypical. But for being editor of this magazine, I probably would have reacted the same way.

In no way did he mean to suggest that the gospel has only to do with the spiritual dimension of life or that the extent and persistence and depth of poverty in the world are irrelevant to the good news of the kingdom of God. Nor would he have disputed the notion that systems can work evil as perversely as individuals — and often more effectively.

And he would agree, I'm certain, with the claim that speaking and acting against the injustice and evil perpetrated by economic structures is every bit as appropriate and important for the church as denouncing and resisting militarism or apartheid or human rights violations.

Many involved and concerned Christians are willing to leave ecumenical commentary and action on the international financial system to specialists and experts. By contrast, the churches' engagement in what we think of as "political" matters — though hardly free from its own difficulties — usually arouses much wider interest.

Despite the obstacles to resolving differences, the issues at stake and the points of disagreement among Christians seem clearer and easier to explain in the arena of politics than in the economic domain.

Not that economics and politics are neatly separable. Economic issues lie at the root of many conflicts, and political oppression and economic domination often go hand in hand.

Yet I suspect that I am not unusual in believing that it's important to find time to read the newspaper every day but invariably skipping over the business and finance section.

The report I refer to makes a convincing case for the ecumenical relevance of mysteries like currency exchange and interest rates, protective tariffs and the International Monetary Fund. It allows few illusions about the possibilities for the churches to speak and act meaningfully in this area, but leaves little doubt that they ought to be trying.

What has to happen, the report says, is a "demystification" of international financial structures — a recognition that, despite their complexity, the issues at stake here are too important to be left to the experts. What worries me more than the intellectual challenge of such a process of "demystification" is the strong suspicion that it might be very uncomfortable.

In a 1961 preface to his *Screwtape Letters*, C. S. Lewis wrote that "the greatest evil is not now done . . . in concentration camps and labour camps. In those we see its final result. But it is conceived and ordered (moved, seconded, carried and minuted) in clean, carpeted, warmed and well-lighted offices by quiet men with white collars and cut fingernails and smooth-shaven cheeks who do not need to raise their voice."

"Amen!" I want to say. But the word sticks in my throat when I realize how much I enjoy the benefits of the quiet decisions made in those offices.

August/September 1985

FAMILY PICTURES

It's that time of year. The film-processing counter at the local super-market is advertising special prices for converting "treasured family snapshots" into Christmas greeting cards. Again it's safe to predict that our family won't take advantage of the offer. Never yet has a camera caught the six of us simultaneously projecting the look of relaxed cheerfulness we'd like distant friends to associate with us.

Older and fading family pictures, preserved in albums that only seldom come out of the closet, suggest that this ideal of relaxed cheerfulness was not what photographers strove for a couple generations ago. Cameras were large and clumsy then, picture-taking a rare event that involved the services of a professional. Posed and shot and produced with care, those photographs were a far cry from what we call (more accurately perhaps than we realize) "snapshots".

A picture is worth a thousand words, we're told. I sometimes wonder. Based on the equivalent of a few thousand such pictorial words about my ancestors, I'm not convinced that they were really the uniformly austere and formidable people who emerge from those photographs.

The question of what family pictures say arises from a WCC programme of ecumenical team visits around Latin America. Most of those who participated in those visits will probably not meet each other again. Memories will surely linger, letters may be exchanged, prayers for each other will be offered. And surely that's not to be underestimated.

For nearly all of the rest of us, however, the stories and pictures of these visits evoke a part of the family we've never seen and never will see. Like the sepia-toned photographs of my great grandparents, they may raise more questions than they answer.

Some will be inclined to ask questions about the real ecumenical importance of these visits. That is surely a legitimate question, but we should not be too quick to answer it. Those who have listened to parables about mustard seeds and treasure buried in fields cannot afford to rule out the possibility that unspectacular occasions like small-scale ecumenical visits might even be signs of the kingdom.

The unfamiliar family pictures on our cover are more than just pointers to the specific incarnations of Christian fellowship which they recall. In illustrating the long tradition of Christian hospitality, the tokens of those visits invite us to ask ourselves how hospitable we are. For if we can think of the pictures on this month's cover as our family pictures, it follows that only a very small part of the family is pictured there.

The writer to Hebrews no doubt had in mind the Old Testament account of Abraham and his divine visitors (Genesis 18 and 19) in saying that showing hospitality to strangers opens up the possibility of entertaining angels unawares (Hebrews 13:2).

The word "angel" comes from the Greek word for "messenger". In a sense, then, the question of hospitality is: are we opening ourselves to all the messages that might be available to us from the strangers-within-our-family?

November 1985

STORY AND INTERPRETATION

Last December a friend enclosed a newspaper clipping with his Christmas card.

The article reported a biblical scholar's claim that the idea of Jesus being born in a stable, to which Joseph and Mary had been banished by an unsympathetic innkeeper, is a misunderstanding. Over many years in the part of the world where Jesus was born, this scholar has closely studied the life and customs of peasants there.

His argument is based on both linguistic and cultural grounds. The Greek word usually translated as "inn" is more correctly understood, according to this scholar, as a general term for a dwelling, lodging or guest room. Ordinary homes of that time, he says, consisted of a large living room raised above ground level, connected to a lower section, in which the family's animals stayed at night. That part of the room typically included a manger.

Furthermore, Bethlehem was Joseph's family home. That's why he went there for the census, the gospel of Luke tells us. Surely he would have had relatives in the town. And, given the strong tradition of hospitality in the Middle East, those kinsfolk would have been deeply insulted if Joseph had taken his pregnant wife to an inn rather than staying with them.

The merits of the overturning of an image that has grown familiar from centuries of carols and Christmas cards I'm not competent to judge.

I do know enough about newspapers to allow for the likelihood that the account presented in the clipping my friend sent me has smoothed out some of the intricacies of the scholarly argument. (The journalist's opening paragraph suggests that Jesus' birthplace was "the Palestinian equivalent of a two-bedroomed, semi-detached house".)

And I know enough about biblical scholarship to suspect that not everyone will be as eager to embrace this new interpretation as one theologian quoted in the new story, who said that "the traditional inn-and-stable scene succeeds only in distancing Jesus" and that it's much more real to think that "Jesus was born in a real, live, warm, loving, crowded home, just as any other Jewish boy might expect to be".

In any case, there's a lesson here about stories and their interpretation. For if the "inn-and-stable scene" indeed distances Jesus from many of us, it also draws a sharp and salutary contrast — particularly when read alongside the account in Matthew about the perplexity at the palace in Jerusalem when the Magi arrived looking for a king — between earthly notions of power and importance and the ideal of power in the gospel.

Suppose, however, that the account in the newspaper clipping is correct. What if Jesus had been born in what sounds very much like a middle-class home? Some of us might find it easier to "identify with him". And after all, isn't the point that he was "one of us" a key to the profound importance of the incarnation?

Of course, there is clearly something offensive in the idea of "claiming" Jesus for our own group — especially when that claim almost inevitably blunts the edge of the gospel message of good news for the poor. At the same time, those of us who are not poor need honestly to ask ourselves whether our eagerness to target the meaning of the Christmas story on the poor is not just a convenient way of insulating ourselves from the offence of the gospel — the "for *us* and for *our* salvation" of the creed.

The lesson is that however effective stories may be as pointers to "the truth", stories cannot long be detached from interpretations of them. And when we start interpreting a story, we bring a lot of our own baggage to it.

December 1985

RELEVANCE

Is the church relevant?

In North America back in the 1960s that was a favourite question, usually posed by those who were quite sure the answer was No. Their concern was (not to put too fine a point on it) that if the church didn't meet the needs of the Real World, people would increasingly dissociate themselves from it and it would eventually die out. The church, of course, was not the only institution subjected to the relevance criterion: education was another favourite target.

It seems as if the question of relevance is not raised today quite as often as it once was. That doesn't necessarily mean the concern has gone away. For one thing, slogans and shibboleths have a short shelf life. For another, in the 1980s, being "relevant" to what people need or want from the church is sometimes defined differently because perceptions of what people think they need or want have changed.

Assuming that one measure of relevance is how often one gets mentioned by the news media, there aren't a lot of questions being asked these days about the relevance of the church in some parts of the world. In North America, for example, pastoral letters by Catholic bishops on nuclear weapons and the economy have elicited heated public debate both inside and outside the church. And campaigns organized by television evangelists with lucrative mailing lists have played a clear role in the political drama.

Examples from elsewhere illustrate the church's relevance even more clearly. In the recent change of government in the Philippines, the name of Jaime Cardinal Sin figured in news stories almost as often as those of Mr Marcos and Mrs Aquino. The involvement of the Philippine church in human rights struggles was of course well-documented even before it made the front pages.

A WCC-Caribbean Conference of Churches team visiting Haiti in February 1986 suggested that one cause of the popular uprising that toppled the 28-year regime of the Duvalier family was a new willingness on the part of the Catholic Church in Haiti, inspired by a remark of the pope during his 1983 visit, to take a stand for justice in the misery of that nation.

And no one needs to be reminded of the role of the church in South Africa today. Late last year, church leaders there released a thought-provoking "theological comment on the political crisis" called "The Kairos Document". The Greek word *kairos* in the document's title means "time" — understood as an opportunity. The authors argue that a *kairos* or "moment of truth" has come for the South African apartheid system.

There is a connection between the ability to read the signs of the times, to discern the present of a *kairos*, to know — as Mordecai said to Esther — "whether you have not come . . . for such a time as this" (Esther 4:22), and the ability to act in ways that will be so relevant that even the media will notice.

It detracts nothing from our gratitude for and admiration of the courage of those "relevant" churches to suggest that churches and groups of Christians who are not in the headlines might also be relevant. For the ability to discern a *kairos* and the courage to witness when it comes are gifts of grace. But it is even more difficult to see how to live relevantly as a church when the *kairos* doesn't seem at all evident.

April 1986

TRAVELLING ON

One speaker at the recent consultation at Bad Boll Evangelical Academy on third-world tourism was a former hotel worker from Manila.

He offered a description of the typical tourist in his country: "a good-natured foreigner with a camera, wearing shorts and a sleeveless shirt, riding around in air-conditioned buses, with a lot of money but not too knowledgeable about prices".

Even if you've never been to the Philippines, you probably aren't surprised by the description. Tourists have long been a favourite target for stereotypes and caricatures.

Tourist caricatures explain why, after three-and-a-half years in Geneva, my daughters seem genuinely convinced that all and only American men wear plaid trousers, so that they unfailingly identify anyone thus dressed on the streets of Geneva as an American tourist.

Tourist caricatures explain why, on any given Saturday, I might be heard making the preposterous claim that most of the population of West Germany and the Netherlands is jamming the road that runs by our apartment complex.

Everyone seems to have heard horror stories about those "If this is Tuesday it must be Belgium" package tours which rush around from city to city in buses that might themselves warrant classification among the Seven Wonders of the World.

We once escorted some friends through Geneva's old city at night after they managed to escape their tour group for a couple of hours. Having arrived in Geneva at 8 p.m. and slated to leave already the next morning at 6:30, most of the group saw only the inside of the hotel where they spent the night.

And "Why don't you stop by and see the slides from our trip

to . . ." has a certain familiar ring as the focus for an invitation to a long and not always stimulating evening. (Come to think of it, maybe "focus" is the wrong word.)

What emerged from the Bad Boll consultation was that there's far more to tourism than the clumsiness and lack of sophistication displayed by many tourists and the superficiality of the expectations that their horizons are going to be broadened by taking a tour that has been arranged at every step to prevent their experiences from being too foreign to them.

The deeper analysis that resulted from listening to people from tourist-receiving countries, to representatives of governments and to those in the tourism business demonstrated that the specific problem of tourism in the third world is an extremely complicated issue, hemmed about by many and powerful vested interests.

When tourism is seen less as the occasion for amusement or disgust, and more as a significant contributing factor to environmental degradation, cultural breakdown and even injustice and oppression, one soon hears talk of a "new international tourist order", as several people at Bad Boll suggested.

The record of ecumenical and other calls for other "new international orders" — in economics, in information and communication — promises a long and frustrating struggle. And appeals for "alternative tourism" — though received sympathetically by those who share convictions about the evils of the present situation — made it evident that there isn't even any agreed definition of what "alternative tourism" is.

A statement issued after the meeting pointed to the need for both idealism and realism in framing concrete recommendations about third-world tourism. That statement makes a strong appeal to the churches in countries from which tourists come: "Before you tell us not to be unrealistic, we want you to listen to the cries of people."

It's a common ecumenical exhortation — *"Listen!"* — but no less to the point for all its familiarity. Perhaps one may hope that hearing people's cries about tourism will be more effective than listening to our own chuckles about tourists.

May 1986

ROOT CAUSES

Providing relief to suffering people represents an important part of Christian obedience. It corrects the temptation — scathingly attacked by the Old Testament prophets — to suppose that the rites of formal worship fulfill our duties to God. "Is not *this* the fast I choose: to loose the bonds of wickedness, to undo the thongs of the yoke, to let the oppressed go free, and to break every yoke? Is it not to share your bread with the hungry, and bring the homeless poor into your house?" (Isaiah 58:6-7).

But if we may not brush aside efforts such as these, neither may we see them as enough. To deal only with the manifestations of human suffering is to be confronted by another prophetic word: Jeremiah's warning against "healing the wound of my people lightly" (8:11).

Only if we seek to identify the root causes of hunger in Africa do we validate our efforts to alleviate the suffering it causes. Only if we seek to identify the root causes of the vast increase in the number of refugees in the world do we acknowledge our indignation that our most fervent and earnest humanitarian efforts help only a fraction of those refugees and them only partially.

This task of identifying root causes is not an academic exercise undertaken in splendid isolation from what the victims of hunger and displacement are saying. The voiceless must have a voice in those discussions of "root causes". And that means more than merely listening to and recording their stories, snapping heart-rending photographs of the misery in which they live, being ourselves moved to tears by their cries. Identifying "root causes" is not an exercise in weaving analytical theories out of somebody else's personal testimonies.

ROOT CAUSES

There's something deceptively easy about speaking of root causes. The importance of identifying them trips a little too lightly off our tongues. The outlines and lists we make accumulate the portentous weight of ecumenical language and issues in yet another imposing document. Eventually, perhaps, the document is edited down and spruced up into something that sounds prophetic. And then what?

To have discovered the cause of a disease is not yet to have cured it. To have prescribed a cure is not yet to have administered it.

June 1986

WATCH YOUR LANGUAGE

"Third-World Tourism" was the title I chose. A colleague from India asked: "Shouldn't you really have said: 'Tourism *in the third world*'?"

A Latin American friend had a problem with the title which re-arranging the word order wouldn't have solved. "Why", she wondered, "do you have to use the term 'third world' — especially in a magazine called *One World?*"

My initial response was that the organization sponsoring the meeting out of which the story grew is called the Ecumenical Coalition on *Third-World Tourism* — formed by church representatives from Africa, Asia, the Caribbean, Latin America, the Middle East and the Pacific.

Fair enough, maybe. But the larger question remains. Should *One World* use the term "third world"?

Granted, it's not ideal. It isn't very specific, for one thing. There's no official list of "third-world" regions or countries or peoples. I once heard a Canadian say that, given the economic and cultural and political domination of its neighbour to the south, Canada is a third-world country. Quite apart from his point about US-Canadian relations, it seems clear that stretching "third world" to include Canada doesn't do much to tighten up the meaning of the phrase.

More importantly, even if one had a list of "third-world countries", the term obscures all the many economic, political and cultural differences among those countries. Don't the negative consequences of lumping together that diversity outweigh the advantages of having a short and simple expression?

It's of course the simplicity that is appealing. Any shorthand is welcome for already too long ecumenical sentences. If the term lacks precision, so do a lot of other words we use. If it blurs certain distinctions, isn't the relevant question whether those distinctions are important in the particular context in which one is using the term?

There's a more subtle problem with the term "third world". It's derived from the French *tiers monde,* that the dictionary says was originally meant to specify countries not aligned with either of the two superpower blocs.

But the ordinary use of the phrase today has gone beyond that original definition of political nonalignment. In the process, doesn't the word "third" carry with it the hint that the counting — which inevitably suggests ranking — is being done from somebody else's perspective?

Some might counter the complaint that their use of the term "third world" offends or demeans the groups it means to describe by arguing that they don't mean to do so. One might go so far as to say, with Lewis Carroll's Humpty Dumpty, that "when *I* use a word, it means just what I choose it to mean — neither more nor less."

We're all tempted by that principle from time to time — to excuse ourselves for having said something offensive or to facilitate a verbal agreement to avoid confrontation. But the price of having a private language is communication strain, if not breakdown.

There is evidence aplenty of how the words we use carry along with them a lot of freight. Our language always has overtones and undertones as well as tones.

Readiness to respect others' sensibilities about our language does not mean giving everyone else an automatic veto over any word we use. What bothers some people may seem trivial to others. On the other hand, if the only sensibilities we respect are those which correspond to our own, we can hardly take credit for much sensitivity.

I'm still not certain how to answer the question I started with. Perhaps moving from "it means just what I choose it to mean" to "I never thought of it that way" is at least a first step towards a better vantage point from which to watch our language.

July 1986

SUPERLATIVELY ECUMENICAL

Journalists do well to be wary of absolute claims and superlatives. Too often one learns, after writing that X is the first of his or her country, confession or sex to hold a certain position or receive a particular honour, that Y achieved the same distinction a year earlier.

Still, the temptation to use superlatives is great. Most of us find them fascinating. The *Guinness Book of World Records* is a perennial best-seller; and it has become commonplace for people actively to seek a place in the record book by undertaking a feat for which no precedent exists.

Some of these sorties at the frontiers of human achievement even attain the status of "news". A wire service report the other day told of a Welshman who spent 100 hours in a vat of baked beans. He raised an unspecified amount of money for an unnamed charity, but more importantly he surpassed by 28 hours the existing Guinness-certified record for "sitting in liquid food".

Two "superlatives" stand out in this issue of *One World*. July's International Conference for Itinerant Evangelists, held in Amsterdam and sponsored by the Billy Graham organization, is said to have been the "most geographically diverse event in history". Elsewhere the WCC Faith and Order Commission, on which a dozen Roman Catholics sit, is described as "the most representative theological body in the Christian world".

The Graham association based its superlative on statistics showing that the 8000-plus evangelists at its conference came to Amsterdam from 173 countries. That's more people from more nations than attended the WCC's sixth assembly, itself sometimes called the most broadly representative meeting in the history of the church. Amsterdam '86 may have been less "balanced" than Vancouver '83 in terms of confessional participation, but persons from virtually every church tradition were present.

In a recent issue of *The Banner* published by the Christian Reformed Church in North America, editor Andrew Kuyvenhoven writes that for many "evangelical" people, who see "evangelists as presenting generic Christianity rather than the brand-name thing offered by denominations", these "big-name evangelists take the place of the ecumenical movement".

Kuyvenhoven has high regard for Graham's work and integrity. But he is uneasy — "biblically, confessionally, church-government-ally" — that it was an individual like Graham instead of the churches together who set up the Amsterdam meeting. He suggests that "if the World Council of Churches did the things churches should do together", the WCC would have brought 8000 evangelists to one place. (The price-tag for the ten-day Amsterdam event, one may note in passing, was about the same as the WCC's 1985 operating budget.)

No doubt the ecumenical movement is not always as clear as it ought to be about the place of evangelism (which Vancouver called "the test of our ecumenical vocation") or about the relationship between mission and unity. But to talk about what "churches should do together" is to be reminded that proclaiming the gospel cannot be isolated from a vast range of things the churches are called to undertake together — the search for visible unity, the search for diakonia, the search for church renewal, the search for a mutual commitment to justice, peace and the integrity of creation.

In these areas of "common witness", superlatives are misleading. Bigger isn't necessarily better; quantity isn't the same as quality. At the same time, small isn't always beautiful. What's important is not whether maximum geographical spread outweighs optimal theological representativeness. But the results do matter — whether of massive get-togethers of evangelists or of doctrinal explorations by Faith and Order's diverse traditions or of any other ecumenical encounter, large or small, that brings Christians together in order better to fulfill, as the WCC Basis says, "their common calling".

October 1986

FREEDOM TO PREACH

It's probably not surprising that Gamaliel's name surfaced from time to time during the recent ecumenical meetings on new religious movements. If ever a "NRM" upset the religious authorities, it was the one born on Pentecost nearly 2000 years ago.

As recorded in Acts 5, Gamaliel comes on stage during a dramatic confrontation with the apostles at a meeting of the Sanhedrin, the council of religious leaders. Sprung from jail in the middle of the previous night, the apostles had their freedom cut short by their immediate return to the place where they had gotten into trouble and their immediate resumption of what they had been told not to do: preaching the gospel and attracting crowds of adherents.

Peter was in anything but a conciliatory mood. His first sentence has become a classic statement of the justification of civil disobedience: we're bound to obey God rather than men. Then, in no uncertain terms, he told the Sanhedrin what obeying God meant to the apostles: proclaiming that the God of *our* ancestors has raised from the dead and exalted Jesus, whom *you* killed. . . .

Some council members wanted to kill the apostles on the spot. But Gamaliel moved to go into closed session instead. He made a speech; there was some discussion; and the apostles were called back, flogged and released.

The core of Gamaliel's speech is familiar: "If this plan or this undertaking is of men, it will fail, but if it is of God, you will not be able to overthrow them. You might even be found opposing God."

Twenty centuries of church history have spawned enough movements of each of Gamaliel's two types to lend a certain plausibility to his line of reasoning. Bizarre heterodoxies that died unmourned on the vine are balanced by the stories of movements that suffered for teachings and practices which once threatened the mainstream but have long since become part of the common Christian heritage.

With the benefit of hindsight not available to the harried Sanhedrin (not to mention the supposition that Our Side prevailed in this episode), we may be inclined to think kindly of Gamaliel. It's a little complicated, though, to apply his advice to the contemporary encounter of the church with new religious movements.

What Gamaliel said had a theological ring (we don't want to oppose God and projects he doesn't bless will fail anyway), but it's basically a tactical suggestion about what happens if those who have a belief they're willing to kill for encounter those who have a belief they're willing to die for. Gamaliel's advice is directed to those who have a certain kind of power at their disposal.

Except for the horrifying case of Jim Jones — who was willing both to kill and to die for what he believed — the stakes don't usually seem that high these days. Still, when faced with the apparent success and power of NRMs today, many Christians seek a response that is effective and powerful. In many cases they have tried to "defend the faith" with the power of the law and of civil authorities.

Ecumenically, Christians have begun to talk more about "powerlessness" recently. In some places, of course, powerlessness has long been a daily reality for those who profess faith in Christ. Elsewhere, it's still something that has to be learned with difficulty — sometimes with the help of the heirs of what is called the "Radical Reformation", itself a NRM that suffered under the power at the disposal of Christians of earlier times.

We can argue about whether Gamaliel was right or wrong. It's less comfortable to ask whether his way of putting the issue is even relevant to how we respond to NRMs.

November 1986

BOREDOM

A pained and thoughtful letter from a reader (now a former reader) wonders "why it is that ecumenical affairs should be so dull".

Testifying to his own ecumenical commitment, the writer says he has been enriched by taking part in cooperative worship and action in his own country and elsewhere. But he finds it increasingly hard to muster the enthusiasm necessary to follow accounts of what is being done ecumenically — at the local level, nationally, and by the World Council of Churches. Too often the accounts simply aren't interesting. He regrets that, but . . .

I understand his guilty conscience over not finding interesting that which he believes to be important. More than once I've lugged home from the library a weighty tome on a significant subject on which I am appallingly uninformed. Two weeks later it goes back, with only the first few pages read.

Particularly where the church is seen as one among many "voluntary organizations" competing for people's commitment, the charge of being uninteresting is worrisome. Surely the "electronic church" succeeds in part because of the care TV preachers devote to entertaining viewers, recognizing that they are only a switch of the dial away from being shut out of anyone's living room.

For an institution like the WCC, a US journalist suggested during the "communicating the WCC" presentation at the January central committee meeting, being ignored by the media is even worse than getting "bad press". And seeming dull or uninteresting is surely to risk being ignored.

Of course, "interesting" is a subjective judgment, varying not only across but within cultures. I may find an evening in a baseball stadium

57

endlessly fascinating. Having been there will, if anything, increase my eagerness the next day to read accounts of the very game I watched. An evening at the opera no doubt evokes similar reactions from many of those who attend it. And a lot of people at the ballpark and the opera house will judge the enthusiasms of those in the other place incomprehensible.

A US psychologist recently made what is said to be the first scientific study of what makes for boredom. Analyzing the results of a student survey, he came up with a list of nine "truly monotonous behaviour patterns", among them "negative egocentrism" (constantly complaining about one's life), self-preoccupation, trying too hard to be nice, and over-seriousness.

Even without the benefit of research, it's not too difficult to hazard a few obvious (and perhaps for that reason not very interesting) generalizations about why the ecumenical movement and the material it produces are not always interesting.

In many ways the ecumenical movement takes shape in institutions (among them the WCC). Institutions are less interesting than people. And what is interesting about interesting people is seldom their institutional connections.

Inevitably, a good deal of what the ecumenical movement does, particularly on the international level, comes to expression in meetings. Participants often find meetings not very interesting. It's a common cliché that what's really important about meetings happens outside of formal sessions — over coffee or lunch or in the corridors.

And just as accounts of an event are almost always less interesting than the reality of it, so, too, reading about a meeting is rarely more interesting than attending it (though it may have the advantage of taking less time).

The efforts to overcome division on the road to unity may blunt or qualify the sharp — and interesting — edges some people would give to some issues. And an emerging ecumenical consensus on an issue may mean that a new statement on an old topic is "nothing new".

For those eager to share the ecumenical vision with others, convinced that life and death issues are at stake, the institutions and meetings and rhetoric in which the movement comes to expression may dampen enthusiasm. Too often, to borrow the apostle Paul's image, our "earthen vessels" *are* uninteresting, concealing treasure rather than conveying it. The yawning gap between what is claimed and what is done will leave a lot of people merely yawning.

At the same time there is a risk in overestimating the importance of being interesting. We may — as the title of a recent book about the triviality of television and its consequent trivialization of social and intellectual life suggests — "amuse ourselves to death".

March 1987

JUST TV?

A newspaper feature article not long ago profiled a 16-year-old US actress who has become well known by appearing in a popular comedy series about an upper-middle-class black family. Next year, she will star in her own TV series.

Lately, however, she's been in the news for her part as a "voodoo priestess" in a film whose graphic portrayals of ritual sex and violence earned it a rare "X" rating in the US (no one under 18 admitted) until it was re-edited to appease industry censors.

The director of the controversial film, admitting to some qualms about choosing a teenager from a family TV series to play the part of a voodoo priestess, rationalized that "what she represents" in the TV show "was maybe a role model for young black American kids; but in the end, if she is going to be the best role model, the way to do it is to be the best actress".

She herself was more down to earth, justifying her role in the film as something that would be good for her career. She added that "there is so much more in life than show business. It's only going to last for so long, but the work that I'm doing with my guru and meditation is forever. . . . I'm much more interested in working on my soul than on my bank account."

Responding to criticisms that the fictional black family in the TV programme in which she plays is "too rich" and "not black enough", she uttered what the feature-writer calls "the wisest words of all": "You want reality? Turn on the news. My God, it's just TV!"

Articles about celebrities, even in newspapers with pretensions to seriousness, are probably best understood as a cog in the public relations machinery that cranks out celebrities — whom someone once

60

defined as "people who are famous not for what they've done but who are famous just for being famous". (After all, how else would ordinary journalists get a chance to interview media idols?) Such articles probably shouldn't be taken too seriously.

The Caribbean Conference of Churches — like many church and other groups elsewhere — is worried about the way television stars operate as "role models".

Their term for "role models" from outside is "cultural penetration"; they're alarmed at the proportions it's reached in their region; and they note with dismay the resulting damage to "human dignity" and "Caribbean values".

"My God, it's just TV!" one might be tempted to exclaim. Granted, the values of diversion and entertainment which the mass media provide are sometimes underestimated by those of a more serious cast of mind.

Nevertheless, before dismissing television's baleful effects as completely ephemeral, one should recall that business people, ordinarily hard-headed about how they spend their money, invest vast sums of money in TV advertising — suggesting that they, at least, believe the medium to be more than "just TV".

The churches, speaking ecumenically at the WCC's sixth assembly in Vancouver, warned that "the new electronic media will enlarge and confirm the global domination of a few countries and make it almost irreversible". To recognize the problem — and to frame it in such strong, even apocalyptic, terms — is of course a long way from proposing solutions that will help the Caribbean, the Pacific or any other part of the world exposed to satellite-beamed glamour and greed.

The 16-year-old actress is correct. There *is* "more to life than show business". Alas, the values and perceptions that show business conveys may in fact last even longer than the work that media role models do "on their souls" with meditation and gurus.

April 1987

COMPARATIVELY SPEAKING

"You can't compare apples and oranges", warns an old cliché. Of course, you can — especially at the end of a meal when someone offers you a choice between the two fruits for dessert.

"Comparison are odious", according to an oft-repeated dictum of one John Fortescue (1395-1476). Be that as it may, most of us make them all the time, often at the persistent urging of politicians seeking our vote or of advertisers who want us to buy their product rather than that of a competitor.

But if the conventional wisdom about the defects of comparison needs to be seasoned with common sense when eating and with realism in the everyday world of making choices, that doesn't completely erode the value of these hoary adages.

"Mission in Christ's Way" is the subtitle of the WCC's planned 1989 World Conference on Mission and Evangelism, "Your Will Be Done".

The diversity of tradition and experience brought together in the ecumenical movement ought to warn us against making "Mission in Christ's Way" a kind of theological trump card, a slogan we can claim as a trademark for whatever activities (or theories) we prefer to think of as "authentic mission".

To ignore that warning is quickly to be drawn into making comparisons that are indeed odious: this activity or programme or model is *more* faithful, *more* holistic, *more* important, *more* urgent than that.

We may even sometimes concede that we are making such comparisons on the basis of our own standards — but of course the unspoken assumption is that our standards are *more* appropriate, *more* theologically sound, *more* reasonable, *more* ecumenical than anyone else's.

I suppose it's possible, maybe even tempting, to compare and contrast a comment about taking evangelism seriously with one about taking people seriously. Perhaps some of us may line up — eagerly or reluctantly — on one side or the other. But to take this sort of "either/or" approach (to which comparisons so often give birth) is to end up taking neither seriously.

The church responds to its missionary calling in the late twentieth century in a world that gives special poignancy to that haunting verse in Luke's gospel: "When the Son of man comes, will he find faith on earth?" (Luke 18:8).

In many places these days the evidence seems all too abundant for a disheartening, if not utterly negative, answer to that question. In any case, it highlights the importance and urgency of taking seriously the mission of the church.

Some interpreters point out that this verse is added to the end of Jesus' parable about a poor woman who finally receives her due by wearing down a corrupt judge with her pleas for justice. The question, they suggest, is as much about faithfulness as about faith.

When the Son of man comes, will he find people with the kind of faithful persistence against all odds that the woman in the parable demonstrates? And, we might add, will he find the church taking those people seriously?

Maybe the larger problem is how glibly we talk about "the church's agenda" or "the ecumenical agenda". Do we not, particularly when thinking about mission, too often forget that "agenda" means that which is *to be done,* not just that which is to be talked about, analyzed and compared?

June 1987

HOW SHALL WE LIVE?

One of the important ways the church functions, it has been said, is as a "community of moral discourse".

Put in less academic language, this phrase asserts that, since New Testament times, those who accept the gospel and seek to follow Jesus Christ have considered it natural and appropriate to discuss and debate with each other about how they ought to behave in this world. Some of the "moral discourse" that went on in the earliest Christian communities is recorded and reflected in the pages of the New Testament.

Most often, perhaps, such discourse begins as a sharing of perplexity and confusion about life's complexities and ambiguities. By grace, it may end up as an occasion for encouragement and solidarity out of which new insights and new resolutions emerge. Sometimes, too, moral discourse takes the form of judgment; and judgment, unaccompanied by compassion, understanding and readiness to forgive and to be forgiven may break the community.

In any case, though — whether through participating in each other's uncertainty, strengthening each other's resolve or affirming unequivocally that a given action is right or wrong — what is presupposed is that the community of Christians can help us in important ways to make decisions.

In everyday life, of course, this "moral discourse" is usually small-scale and informal. Most of us are much more prone to muddling through, perhaps with the counsel of a small group of friends, than to postponing action until we have carefully worked out a line of moral reasoning derived from agreed ethical principles.

Throughout history the church has often seemed less interested in "moral discourse" than in making rules and monitoring compliance with them. As a result, people — sometimes for noble reasons and with great courage, sometimes out of selfishness — resist the idea that the church is a source of guidance for their behaviour. Determined to say "I did it *my* way", many leave the church or ignore it out of disagreement over moral issues.

When the churches agree ecumenically that they have "a common calling", that has implications in the moral realm as well. Like all "moral discourse", the ecumenical variety is incomplete and imperfect. Its effectiveness may be weakened and its sharp edges dulled by the need to take into account the great diversity of the churches.

Opportunities to wrestle together with what our common faith requires of us are few and far between, and when they happen they are usually all too brief.

Those who participate in such exchanges bring along their own conceptual baggage and their own biases. They may be tempted to absolutize their own experiences and ethical insights — or to take so seriously the experiences and insights of those whom they meet that they offer nothing in return. The records and reports of what happens in the best of such encounters only inadequately reflect their depth.

It may be helpful to see the ongoing ecumenical engagement in the struggle for liberation in South Africa in terms of the church as a community of moral discourse. Meetings like the one organized by the WCC in Lusaka, Zambia, on "The Churches' Search for Justice and Peace in Southern Africa" (May 1987) are links in a chain of solidarity and a means of reminding church and world alike of an important issue of justice and oppression that many would rather forget about. But they are also occasions for the worldwide church to become — briefly and inadequately though it be — a community of moral discourse.

For the Christian community in southern Africa and elsewhere, the struggle to "set at liberty those who are oppressed" includes a profound and painful struggle with very specific and very difficult questions about how we are to live out our confession that Jesus Christ is Lord and that we mean to follow him.

July/August 1987

65

A QUESTION OF OWNERSHIP

It was one of those long conversations with a friend one hasn't seen for several years — a pleasant evening chat that meandered through many subjects.

We exchanged the usual information about what we were up to, about our families, about mutual acquaintances. I have no idea how we ended up talking about united churches.

My friend, a theologian by training and trade, is ecumenically interested and involved. He is quite familiar with one united church; and he is even more closely acquainted with a number of notably un-united churches.

Since his own church tradition has been particularly fissiparous, with more than its share of purists and heresy-hunters, his sense of the importance of church unity is not just a matter of theological conviction. It is also the product of first-hand experience with the unpleasant and un-Christian things that normally happen when biblical mandates about not being "mismated with unbelievers" and "light having no fellowship with darkness" turn into slogans for schismatics.

Yet the united church he knows well troubles him. "It seems as if anything goes," he explained. "You can believe anything — or you can believe nothing. There appear to be no traditions, no standards by which to measure what it means to belong to such a church. And I'm not sure if it's a good idea to have ecumenical fellowship with a church like that."

The issue of the limits on what one may believe and still be considered part of the church is as old as Christianity itself. And the question of fellowship with churches that do not exhibit all of what one believes to be the marks of the church was on the agenda at the very beginning of the modern ecumenical movement. Not surprisingly, our evening's discussion over dinner didn't go much further than restating the questions.

My friend's familiarity with one united church raises theological problems to which he has given a great deal of thought. Other components of the phenomenon of united churches and those seeking to unite more often occasion cynicism than serious reflection.

The real impediments to church union, on this jaded view, are power and money. Who is going to be selected — or passed over — for staff positions in the new denomination? What will happen to the pension plan for clergy and other church employees?

Naturally, everyone is in favour of saving resources by eliminating duplication of programmes. But fewer people are eager to lose their own jobs in the process. As a result, church union negotiations may end up seeming as long, complex and frustrating as superpower disarmament talks.

We touched on these issues, too, in our inconclusive conversation. But I'm struck now that there was an entire area of difficulties with united and uniting churches that we hadn't talked about.

These are the difficulties faced by churches seeking union in areas of the world where the things that divide Christians have been imported from outside. And financial power can play a divisive role here, too. A church that unites with another, for example, may run the risk of losing bilateral support in carrying out its mission or even subsidizing the salaries of its pastors.

What is at stake is not just tidying up church administration and making structures more rational, but the very witness of the church. That can raise particular problems in a country like Indonesia, where Christians are a small minority.

Bishop Leslie Boseto of the United Church of Papua New Guinea and the Solomon Islands has put his finger on a critical issue here: that of *ownership*. The impasse will remain "unless and until we are 'owned by the owner', rather than our trying to own God by denominationalizing, doctrinalizing, institutionalizing and racializing him".

It's an uncomfortable thought that many of us may be doing just that when we talk about "our" church — and that the heterodoxy of that may be far more serious than many of those found in what seem to us to be "anything-goes" united churches.

September 1987

67

SHARING THE SUFFERING

"If one member suffers, all suffer together," says Paul in his first letter to the Corinthians (12:26).

Cast in the form of an aphorism, the words tend to become a slogan that trips lightly from our tongues. They shouldn't.

To impress on the fractious congregation at Corinth the need to overcome their divisions, Paul compares the church of Jesus Christ to a body. Just as a human organism has a variety of parts with different functions, so the members of the church receive, from "one and the same Spirit", a variety of gifts.

The diversity — some able to heal, others to prophesy, some to speak wisely, others to speak in tongues — is a blessing. It must not lead to discord, Paul insists. If it does, the organization that the organism requires will break down.

The way God has endowed the body which is the church, Paul suggests, mirrors how the human body is composed. Thus, the members must "have the same care for one another" as they do for themselves. If one suffers, all suffer together; if one rejoices, all are happy together.

It's a fairly straightforward comparison. The generalizing of pain in the human body doesn't need much argument, as nearly anyone can attest by thinking back to his or her most recent toothache.

The extended family of the local congregation will often experience the application of Paul's image in the sharing of joy and suffering, especially at times of bereavement.

On a wider scale, it's not difficult to find examples of how bad things in one area have an effect elsewhere. When one US television evangelist was recently brought down in a wave of scandal, popular confidence in all other media preachers was shaken as well.

More serious examples are evident in what are sometimes optimistically described as "regional conflicts", which constantly threaten to spread, drawing in even those other countries which would be hard pressed to declare which of the two sides they favoured.

The international debt crisis has made it clear that the weaknesses of the global economic system threaten the economically powerful creditors, as well as the weak and oppressed victims.

But what is the ecumenical "cash value" of Paul's comparison? The apostle's words seem to be tougher than a mere observation about the interlinkings of geopolitics and the fragility of global economics.

"If one member suffers, all suffer together." But what if it isn't *one* member who is suffering, but hundreds or thousands or millions: tortured or oppressed, jobless or in despair, starving or hungry or diseased. Do all of us really suffer together?

So should we aspire to *suffer* along with Surinamese displaced by internal strife in their country, or with expatriate Haitians living in misery on the sugar plantations of the Dominican Republic or in fear of immigration officials in the US? If we really could make their *suffering* our own, wouldn't we in fact reduce any opportunity to do anything about the conditions that make them suffer?

The mystery of suffering — why anyone should suffer, why some should suffer and others do not — is, of course, a theological puzzle that goes back to the Book of Job and beyond. And because it is such a mystery, any call to share in the suffering of others runs the great risk of being either naive or pathological on the one hand, or trivial and insulting on the other.

So, we need to be cautious when we cite Paul's words, "if one member suffers, all suffer together", even if their truth does not depend on our exemplifying them.

Instead of wondering whether we can suffer along with others, perhaps we should first ask ourselves why, if the church is really a body whose members "have the same care for one another", we so seldom feel anything at all when its members are suffering.

October 1987

LANGUAGE THAT RINGS TRUE

"Be with us, Lord, on our wayward home." That delightful spoonerism from a prayer at the end of a meeting has stuck in my mind for years.

(This arbitrary perversity of memory is an enduring fascination. Why should such an utterly trivial fragment of an experience resurface again and again long after the event, although its context is lost and far more significant impressions from, say, two weeks ago have disappeared forever?)

I heard that prayer during the declining days of what we used to call the "language of Zion", those solemn and often sonorous oratorical cadences considered appropriate, if not mandatory, when praying, preaching or speaking in general about the Christian faith.

Perhaps unnatural phrases like "our homeward way" — the expression that the person giving the closing prayer long ago didn't get quite right — were used because their very remoteness carried with it a hint that it is indeed fitting "to bring before the Throne of Grace" one's semi-conscious anxieties that one might encounter engine breakdown, errant drivers, damaging weather or assorted muggers and bandits as one made one's way home through the night.

In those days, a hotly debated issue in some English-speaking churches was whether it was permissible to use the pronoun "you" — rather than the awkward forms of "thou" — in addressing God.

To judge from my own church, at least, that is no longer an issue today. "Progressives" and "conservatives" alike use "you" in their prayers, though doubts are occasionally voiced that the informal chattiness which now so often seems to exemplify the depth of one's personal Christian commitment is in fact an improvement on the "language of Zion".

70

Experiences in the ecumenical movement often provide vivid evidence of the many facets of the language issue. Most obviously it surfaces in the diversity of languages spoken and understood by members of Christian churches around the world — and the complexity and expense of trying to overcome the obvious hindrances to communication (and the less obvious injustices) that language differences produce.

Honesty compels the admission that the ecumenical movement also generates a vast amount of its own jargon, seldom as magnificent as the "language of Zion" but no less foreign-sounding outside the immediate inner circle.

And even when we overcome the in-group terminology and standardized rhetoric, we face the ever-present reminder that what we do and what the church does speak louder than our most eloquent and straightforward testimonies and declarations and statements and resolutions.

Recognizing how often our familiar and traditional language obscures our meaning, conceals our message and blocks our communication can be a first step towards creative efforts to find new language.

Part of what the Popular Image Creation Centre is trying to do among grassroots groups in Brazil involves the medium of video, whose best-known use by Christians has come under a great deal of criticism in the "electronic church".

But as the story from Brazil points out, there is more at issue here than just the *content* of what is being transmitted electronically. The medium has a language of its own. And it's a language that has to be discovered and learned.

Some of the stories of evangelism in Eastern Europe that emerged at a recent WCC-sponsored consultation on that subject also reflect creative efforts to find a different and appropriate language to convey a Christian message in particular social and political situations. Sometimes it's folk music or Bach oratorios, other times it's audiovisual presentations or pantomimes on biblical themes.

Not to be forgotten in the search for an appropriate and communicative language is the warning cited in a story from a Czech pastor who was describing how he involves people in his congregation in telling stories through pantomime. "If you have nothing to say," he says, "don't try to act, because you will ring false."

LANGUAGE THAT RINGS TRUE

Our language does sometimes manage to have a nice ring to it. But does it ring true? Do *we* ring true?

November 1987

REVERSIBLE PROGRESS

I had been in the US Army for two days. Well-meaning friends (few with actual military experience) had prepared me for the worst, but I was a long way from figuring out how to cope with the routinization and robotization by which armies have, from time immemorial, instilled in unwilling recruits the order and servility that basic training requires and develops.

Far from home, friends and a job I liked, I felt myself mired and sinking in Bunyan's "slough of despond" — with 728 of the 730 days of obligatory duty still ahead of me.

Just before lights out, a tough Southern white, who more than matched my every stereotype of an army sergeant, came into the barracks. "Maybe you men want to know some news," he said tersely. (At this stage of training, no one was allowed books, far less newspapers, radios or TV.) "Somebody's killed Reverend King. They're burning down Washington. And if I was there, I'd be burning it down with them. He was a good man."

The reaction in the barracks was a silence deeper than any enforced by an officer's order. It would be flattering to report that the news focused my own depression on something more significant than my personal plight, but I don't recollect making such a distinction. And only later did it strike me that the sergeant's rough response to King's death might require nuancing of my assumption that everyone with authority in the army had an identical point of view on every subject.

That happened twenty years ago this month. A good deal has changed since then. The shock over the murder of Martin Luther King, like the shock at the other political violence that scarred my

73

country in the 1960s, has long since disappeared, recalled only occasionally when someone asks, "Where were you when . . . ?"

Many people suppose that the changes in the racial situation in the US since King's death indicate a certain measure of progress. Not enough, to be sure, and not quickly enough, but steps in the right direction nevertheless. Much remains embedded in the structures of society; too few people have benefited — and most of them too little — from programmes and laws designed to overturn the evils of the past.

Those attracted by that assessment may be profoundly troubled. At a recent meeting called by US commissioners of the WCC's Programme to Combat Racism (PCR) racism was shown to be increasing in the United States, "as if it has suddenly become permissible again to be openly bigoted".

Like the "old racism", this "new" variety targets not only black Americans, but also those of other minority groups — Hispanics, people of Asian and Pacific Island background and, of course, Native Americans, whose suffering has gone on the longest and who have always been the least protected from public racial slurs.

Some may protest that the ecumenical community is once again turning its attention on faults in US society while ignoring (so it is said) injustice and oppression elsewhere.

But keeping score is not what is at issue. No doubt there are many cases of racism around the world that have not drawn the attention of PCR, as there may be facets of the US racial situation that did not emerge in the Los Angeles meeting. What is important is the global link — the reality that as long as anyone anywhere in this one world is suffering for his or her race or colour, none of us can be anything but disturbed — and the lesson we so dislike hearing: that progress in overcoming injustice is not, alas, irreversible.

April 1988

PENTECOST IN THE CITY

When my grandfather emigrated from the Netherlands to California in the early part of this century, the family realized they would probably never see each other again. So they decided to have a family picture taken — a rarity at that time.

One family member, however, is missing on the photograph. Uncle Ewoud, so the story goes, adamantly refused to adjust his plans for working in the fields that day to accommodate the visit of the photographer.

There are two interpretations of this minor family legend. One is that Uncle Ewoud was a self-willed and cantankerous old grouch who simply didn't feel like dressing up in his Sunday best in the middle of the week.

The other explanation sees him as a sturdy peasant who knew that the productivity of the soil — whose cultivation he as a Calvinist would have considered to be his God-given vocation — depended on respect of the rhythms of nature, something that transcended the sentimental attractions of a family portrait.

Was Uncle Ewoud's boycott a consequence of his alienation from his kinfolk? Or did it reflect his appreciation for what could rather be identified as the "integrity of creation"?

Since no one is around to expand on (or for that matter to verify) the story, we'll never know. But the latter explanation is an attractive one, particularly, perhaps, for those who are tempted to romanticize life on the farm.

Nearly every summer while growing up, I spent a couple of weeks or so on various relatives' farms. Years later, I look back on that with a nostalgia that filters out the evidence even a child must have seen that (to use the picture-language of Genesis 3) it is thanks to the sweat of somebody's face that we eat bread.

A study report drafted at a recent WCC consultation on the integrity of creation warns against mistaken approaches to the disintegration of creation.

The report suggests that among the ways in which people, including Christians, go wrong in this area are *reductionism* (shrinking the gospel to the eternal salvation of individual persons and ignoring God's work in the world), *utopianism* (ignoring the ineradicable reality of sin) and *fatalism* (indifference to or despair over the human causes of creation's groaning).

It also warns against *neo-apocalypticism* (welcoming the ecological crisis and nuclear threat as a promise of the nearness of the Second Coming rather than a divine judgment calling us to repentance) and *scientific-technological hubris* (supposing that the ecological crisis is a technical problem that can be solved by technical means).

And the report criticizes what it calls a *"romantic response . . .* , nostalgic for a return to a pre-technological way of life, ignoring the God-given dynamism of science and technology as a force to be brought under human control rather than to be escaped from".

There is something attractive about the "back-to-nature" approach. It's clear that a lot of threats to justice, peace and the integrity of creation are spawned because an increasing percentage of humankind lives in cities. You can discover that in the grinding poverty of *favelas* and in the lonely anonymity of luxury apartments. You can read about it in the writings of sociologists and economists.

You can even see this negative view of cities reflected in the opening chapters of Genesis. The first city is built by Cain, the first murderer. The tower of Babel, whose construction elicits so strong a reaction from the Lord, is the centrepiece of a city that the people decide to build "to make a name for themselves". And a few chapters later we see the hapless Lot moving ever closer to Sodom and Gomorrah.

The account in the Acts of the Apostles of the coming of the Holy Spirit and the birth of the church reverses the Babel story. It is interesting that this story is set in the context of the celebration — in a city — of what was a Jewish agricultural festival. And the city, of course, is

Jerusalem, which appears in the last book of the New Testament as the symbol of the new creation.

May 1988

TRADEMARKS AND TRANSCENDENCE

Some years back there was talk in my denomination about whether to register its name and symbol as a trademark with the appropriate authorities.

The debate, whose outcome I've forgotten, was touched off by concern in some quarters that the way dissident groups were using the denomination's name might lure the unwary into incorrect ideas of what the church officially taught — as hamburger lovers might be led astray if just any restaurant were allowed to adorn its premises with yellow plastic "golden arches".

The term "ecumenical" of course comes with no such protection. Anyone can use the name or claim its aura for a publication, group, activity or programme. (A few years ago the movie *Network* even used "ecumenical" in the name of a violent urban guerrilla group.)

These many different forms of ecumenism might be seen as a far cry from the compelling simplicity of what Jesus prayed for — so often cited as the source of the ecumenical vision: "that they may be one, that the world might believe".

Often committed persons join together, across traditional lines of church division, to confront a need or concern which they see as going unmet by existing church and interchurch structures, including the WCC. Such an experience may encourage some of them to explore other areas of possible ecumenical collaboration; but it seems as likely that overcoming denominational separation will remain something they do as individuals, seeing no particular consequences for the institutional life of their churches.

Some may worry that all this diffusion of the ecumenical spirit has a detrimental effect on strengthening and developing leadership for what they would consider "mainstream" ecumenical life, such as the WCC has represented for forty years.

"Let a hundred flowers blossom," others may say. The ecumenical movement is finally the work of the Spirit, not an exercise in building a superchurch. If its sprawling and disorderly outgrowths don't match our tidy notions, so much the worse for our tidy notions.

Still others would emphasize a far more radical challenge than mere pluralism in the rise of new ecumenical communities outside the "mainstream". Argentine theologian José Míguez Bonino suggests that there is a fundamental twofold division in the life of the church — as in the world as a whole — between domination and solidarity.

Consciously or unconsciously, he says, many ecumenical structures — interchurch aid, confessional organizations, donor agencies, church institutions and other movements — build up a "clientele" and buy their loyalty for purposes that frequently have more to do with the concerns and struggles in Europe and North America than with the life and witness of the churches in the so-called third world.

That isn't the whole picture, of course. "Organizations of human rights, peoples' organizations, small struggling communities have been stimulated, upheld and supported through communication, funds and visits from solidarity organizations and churches in the northern hemisphere."

But the system of domination and the movement of solidarity are not "symmetrical realities". The former, Bonino says, is an established system which makes the rules, assigns the resources, regulates communications and establishes the mechanisms of control. "It operates with a rationality it has developed, and this systemic rationality pervades the whole life of the *oikumene,* from the economic world of the multinationals to the political organizations, the defence systems, the world extension of mass media, and the cultural and religious world bodies, including the WCC.

"On the other hand, we have the movement of solidarity which rests on a qualitatively different logic and rationality: the presence of transcendence, the search for the immanence of the new future latent in reality and, therefore, the search for a praxis which releases this future. This is the rationality of faith, for which the reality of God is more decisive than the reality of the world as it is."

It's not hard to figure out to which sort of rationality seeking a trademark belongs.

June 1988

HAPPY BIRTHDAY?

Anniversaries provoke a spectrum of responses.

At one extreme is a handful of debunkers who, perhaps out of a general disrelish for parties, remind us that we celebrate the passing of 40 or 200 or 1000 years only because we happen to count by the decimal system. These apparently "round" numbers have no cosmic significance.

The stones from the Jordan which twelve men were told to pile up in Gilgal (Joshua 4) had no cosmic significance either. Yet so important was setting up a visual reminder of Yahweh's might for future generations that it warranted delaying the occupation of the Promised Land.

Anniversary events, like those stones, are evocations of the past, pegs on which to hang a sense of history. How we react to being thus reminded will take different forms according to how we develop that sense of history.

The ideal response is probably something like humble thanks for God's grace and renewed resolve to go forward into the future by recapturing the best of the vision and rekindling the best of the ideals concerned in the event commemorated.

The besetting temptation is to exaggerate the past so as to create some reflected glory to bask in. So most anniversary celebrations generate noisy gales of uncritical self-congratulation.

Serious historians seldom get invited to plan these celebrations. They uncover too many inconvenient doubts and questions about the symbolic simplicities that fuel such galas.

But even serious historians often merely repeat in more sophisticated terms the story that the winners have always told. They remind

81

us that our ancestors had feet of clay. Less often do they challenge our willingness to take for granted that *our* ancestors were somehow uniquely important.

Some recent anniversaries have been the occasion for more critical questioning of the myths that legitimate the status quo. This has been the case in the Australian bicentennial celebrations. Latin American Christians, among others, promise to use commemorations of Columbus's voyage planned for 1992 as an opportunity to highlight the suffering today that can be traced back 500 years.

Many Christians outside of Namibia joined in an ecumenical day of prayer in May to express solidarity with the oppressed people of the country on the tenth anniversary of the Kassinga massacre. Reluctant to be accused of raining on somebody else's party, we may find it more awkward to express solidarity with oppressed people in the context of the bicentenary of European settlement of Australia.

Ecumenically speaking, how do those of us who are not part of a group that is celebrating mark an anniversary? Often we can think of nothing more than the obvious response: congratulations or, if the event was a clearly tragic one, expression of solidarity. But in what sense can and do we see the event being remembered as *our* anniversary?

What would it mean for those of us who are not Russians to see the millennium that Christians in the Soviet Union celebrated last month as a commemoration of something significant in and for *our* history? What would it mean for those of us who are not Australians to understand 1788 as part of *our* past as members of the human community?

One could ask the same question about many other anniversaries celebrated in 1988 — the 250th anniversary of the "warming" of John Wesley's heart, the 50th anniversary of the Nazi annexation of Austria, the 40th anniversary of the accession to power of the National Party in South Africa, the 40th anniversary of the establishment of the State of Israel.

July 1988

LEARNING FROM CHILDREN

I can still visualize the pained expression on the face of an old friend, a distinguished teacher of ethics and the philosophy of religion.

It was about an hour before he was scheduled to give an evening lecture (about love and justice, as I recall) at a local church. The pastor's secretary, who had arrived early to attend to arranging chairs and starting the coffee machine, had brought her ten-year-old son along.

Spotting the boy, and suddenly afraid that he had completely misconstrued his speaking invitation, my friend turned to me and said plaintively, "But I didn't write the speech for *children!*"

He needn't have worried too much. Like most churchgoing boys and girls, this one had, by the age of 10, acquired considerable experience of sitting through speeches and sermons which — whatever else they may be — are "not written for children".

Somehow that incident from long ago came to mind in September at the closing service of the Dutch "day for sharing".

As the worship began, the children present sang a song written for the occasion and taught to them during the day. "Let the children go first," said the worship leader, "for they know best."

The WCC's children's art festival on Justice, Peace and the Integrity of Creation grew out of a similar recognition that we adults often compound our ineptitude at *teaching* children by failing to see how we can *learn* from them.

When we talk about learning from children, of course, there is always the risk of falling into what might be called the "Isn't that *sweet?*" trap. Overwhelmed by warm good feelings at, say, a Sunday school Christmas pageant, how often are we really challenged to hear the gospel of the incarnation in a new way?

We do well to be on guard against this persistent temptation to romanticize children. What parent, nerves frayed by squabbling children, would not resent being reminded that when Jesus called little children to him he said "of such is the kingdom of heaven"?

Of course, we understand that when Jesus said "unless you turn and become like children . . ." it wasn't their sibling feuds and fights he had in mind. But what does it mean to say of children that they know *best* and thus to resolve to learn from them about "sharing" or about "justice, peace and the integrity of creation"?

Like my friend's splendid lecture on theological ethics, most of the ecumenical discussion of these issues has not been written for children. Even the vocabulary would sound foreign to their ears. Their instincts about right and wrong, sharply honed in personal experience, are generally uncomplicated by analyses of "structural injustice" and "systems of oppression".

One way of learning from them is indirectly. We see the evil in such systems and structures no more clearly than when we are confronted by what they do to children who are most vulnerable to and victimized by them.

When we read what a Christian from the Philippines or Zambia has to say about the effects of the international debt crisis on children in their countries, it's no longer so easy to dismiss this as just an issue for bankers to worry about and economists to puzzle over.

Even the fears of children whose exposure to suffering is mostly second-hand can serve to remind us how easily we have made our peace with some dreadful realities precisely because we recognize how complicated they are.

More difficult is learning *directly* from children. The best-known of all stories of this kind of learning is probably the age-old fable of the emperor's new clothes.

Are we prepared to subject the elaborate cautions we weave to explain why we are not sharing, or doing justice, or making peace, or preserving the creation, to the clear-eyed simplicity of a child's observation? Maybe the answer to that is a measure of just how ready we are to learn from children.

November 1988

TRUE CHRISTMAS COLOURS

"Well, what would *you* do," a colleague asked, "if you were convinced that someone was the antichrist?"

We were talking about the recent altercation in Strasbourg when the Northern Ireland Protestant minister Ian Paisley interrupted the pope's address to the European Parliament, loudly denouncing him as the antichrist. Security guards physically removed Paisley from the chamber.

No matter what one may think of the Roman Catholic Church, to call the pope "antichrist", the very personification of evil, probably strikes most people as ecumenically embarrassing, if not bizarre, outrageous or even libellous. Moreover, it is rude to interrupt people, the more so a person who is giving a public speech at the invitation of a body of which you are a member.

These immediate reactions lead directly to the puzzling question above. If you really believe someone to be the *antichrist* (and not merely mistaken or misleading or dangerous), then making that belief public, no matter how discourteously, is in fact a fairly mild response. One may go on to ask if such a response is likely to be effective; and if it's ineffective (or even counterproductive) one might argue for some other strategy.

But my friend's puzzling question is also a peculiar one. To be sure, one hears and thinks a lot about evil in our day. And many church and ecumenical statements do not mince words when talking about evil. They speak of "principalities and powers" or even "the Beast". Sometimes they declare that a given manifestation of evil raises a *status confessionis* — an issue on which where you stand determines whether or not you are within the church.

At the same time, we are aware that great evils operate through structures that entangle and implicate most of us. That cautions against denunciations that focus evil too narrowly.

The question of how to respond to the antichrist seems odd and academic, not because we don't recognize evil but because we know too much about its extent to try to focus it on any one person, even symbolically.

We are moved to anger and sometimes resistance by the vile forms oppression has taken in our century — the massacre of Armenians, the holocaust of Nazi Germany, the cancer of racism and wickedness of its legalized entrenchment in apartheid, the greed of those "who join house to house, who add field to field", the brutality of torturers, the ravages of those who despoil nature and refuse to believe that "the earth is the Lord's".

But if reading stories like these outrages us, it seems too "apocalyptic" to centre ultimate evil on one person, whom we call "antichrist".

In the Christmas story in Luke's gospel we hear of a different kind of connection between "antichrist" and "apocalyptic". The aged Simeon follows his song in the temple — which includes those beautiful words "for mine eyes have seen thy salvation" — with some private words to Mary. He warns that the child she is holding is "set for a sign that is spoken *against* . . . so that thoughts out of many hearts may be *revealed*".

This kind of opposition — what can it mean to "speak against a sign"? — has a lower profile than the monstrous evil which the word "antichrist" usually connotes. This kind of revelation ("apocalypse") — of "the thoughts out of many hearts" — is far less dramatic than the visions of the end in the Bible or in a flood of subsequent popular Christian art and literature.

Simeon is saying that how we respond to this "sign" — this "babe wrapped in swaddling cloths and lying in a manger" — shows our true colours.

It's an intriguing theological puzzle to ask, "How would I respond if I believed someone was the antichrist?" More pertinent, perhaps, is to ask, "How do I respond when the thoughts of my heart reveal that I am 'speaking against the sign' of Christmas?"

December 1988

NO CHEAP COMFORT

Coffee break during a meeting at the Ecumenical Centre early in December was a chance to go back to my office to check the mail. It included a letter from a reader in New Zealand, with the news that a mutual friend had been killed in an automobile accident.

The word of his death shattered through the routine of the morning.

The meeting resumed. We turned our attention to the order of the day. Not long before the hour set for adjournment, the everyday-ness of this ordinary Thursday was shattered again: someone came in to tell the General Secretary that Armenian church authorities were now estimating that the earthquake the previous day had taken 85,000 lives.

Under the circumstances, the meeting's routine agenda suddenly seemed not urgent or relevant enough to continue. After a brief prayer, we filed out silently.

Inevitably, these two items of news about death in the space of single morning set off the sort of reflection which one is generally inclined to avoid.

Unable to face the scope of human suffering and too accustomed to having it quantified for us in the daily news, we are often shocked or stunned, but seldom pained. But when news of the death of thousands of nameless people far away comes at the same time as news of the death of one individual who somehow touches us personally, it strikes us in a new way.

In the end, of course, the mystery remains. We are tempted to speculate about the mathematics of grief, but the thought of a single person's death does not ultimately help us — as we may at first think — to grasp the scale of the tragedy of whole villages being wiped off the map. Nor is there any real comfort in learning later that the death toll in an earthquake may have been closer to 25,000 than 85,000.

It is a token of our inability to understand such realities that churches and philanthropic agencies ministering in situations of mass suffering and dying are often first confronted with a clamour to "*do* something, never mind what" and then with a phenomenon called "donor fatigue", a sort of benumbed paralysis of the diaconal instinct.

A Dutch Christian TV producer made a related point in conversation with a group of ecumenical communicators recently. Fewer and fewer people, he said, will watch yet another film about suffering and dying somewhere else in the world — unless it is somehow linked with a personal struggle in that situation on the part of an individual with whom they can identify.

The subject of death — whether of one person or many — is fraught with puzzles and uncertainties and most of all, perhaps, fear. It's sometimes said that death is the last taboo subject.

In fact, however, a good deal has been written and said about it. Some of it is moving, most is well-intentioned, but little seems finally to come to terms with death. Nevertheless, phrases like "the forces of death" or "merchants of death" slip easily into our rhetoric.

But if we acknowledge that the last word has not been spoken about death, this season of the church year reminds us again of the Christian affirmation that death does not have the last word. At "the intersection of life and death" — in the words of Stanley Samartha, the first director of the WCC's sub-unit on Dialogue with People of Living Faiths and Ideologies — we are challenged not to miss the resurrection.

The temptation is to let the truth of the resurrection slip into the same sort of abstraction as our general thoughts about death. The last chapter of the gospel of Mark — in what biblical scholars say was its original abrupt form — corrects such cheap comfort.

The women, we are told, come to the tomb and find it empty. An angel tells them that Jesus has arisen. Their response is to flee from the tomb, saying not a word to anyone, *"for they were afraid"*. And there the gospel-writer ends the story.

Perhaps imagining that we can enjoy the comfort of resurrection without fear is not so different from supposing that we can really understand death.

March 1989

HAVE YOU HEARD THE STORY ABOUT . . . ?

The mayor of a large US city achieved lifetime tenure with the aid of a well-oiled party machine apt at dispensing favours and (so opponents charged) stuffing ballot boxes.

His electoral invincibility led detractors to imagine a boat trip on which the mayor was joined by the president of the United States and the pope.

A violent storm came up; and it was soon evident that the craft was large enough for only one of the three to survive. Like the sailors bound with Jonah for Tarshish, they began an urgent discussion of who should be jettisoned.

The pope started by pressing his claim not to be thrown overboard, based on his status as bishop of Rome, which is to say, supreme pontiff of the Catholic Church — a primacy he was quite prepared under the circumstances to extend to all of the world's billion or so Christians.

"Obviously, I should be the one to be saved," countered the president. "After all, I am the Leader of the Free World." (The story dates from a time when such rhetorical flourishes met fewer objections than they might today.)

"Well, this is a *democracy*," the mayor said. "The majority rules. Why don't we vote on which of us should be saved?"

The other two agreed. A secret ballot was taken; and when the votes were tallied, the mayor had won the three-way race with 3 votes for the mayor, to 1 for the president, to 1 for the pope.

The relevance — some would even say the "truth" — of such stories has nothing to do with whether or not they happened. Rather, it lies in the way "losers" use their bold simplifications to cut through the obfuscations of "winners", particularly those who think they should justify the ploys which keep them in power.

Political jokes, which flourish in cheerless societies where abuse of power is endemic, are vehicles for conveying messages that do not so easily penetrate through detailed and documented factual accounts and analyses.

Of course, this strength is also a limitation. An anecdote that tries to take into consideration all the complexities and ambiguities of a situation, which seeks to "give the devil his due" or even to tell "the other side of the story", is quite literally "pointless".

A political joke is meant to be laughed at. Such laughter may indicate the triumph of the human spirit over adversity. But it may also represent a hollow and fatalistic cynicism.

Testimonies of personal suffering at the hands of misused power — several of which appear in this issue as well — go a step further. They turn abstractions like "oppressive social structures" or *"intifada"* into accounts of what is happening to our flesh-and blood fellow human beings.

By looking at a vast conflict through the eyes of an individual or family caught up in it, such testimony can help us to "identify with" the victims of injustice, to put ourselves in their place, to commit ourselves to solidarity with them and to the infinitely more difficult search for ways to express our solidarity. We may be moved to tears of anger or frustration; but we will not so easily respond with the bitter cynicism a joke may elicit.

April 1989

THE BIBLE GAP

Long after medieval theologians had quite sensibly moved on from calculating how many angels could dance on it, the pinhead found another unusual use: as a place for skilled miniaturists to inscribe the entire Lord's prayer.

This triumph of human ingenuity wedded to superhuman patience might earn the perpetrator a place in travelling museum exhibits or the "Believe It Or Not!" columns of the popular press. But having little practical or devotional value, it remained a curiosity.

In due time it was outdone by technology. I recall writing a feature story twenty-odd years ago on "the world's smallest Bible", reduced to the dimensions of a microfiche card that some firm had donated to our college.

That, too, shrinks into insignificance when compared with the CD-ROM ("Compact Disk — Read Only Memory") Bible. According to a press release that came across my desk not long ago, a single compact disk (which sells for about US$1,400) can store the text of six English, a French, a German and two Spanish Bibles, Hebrew and Greek originals (transliterated into Roman characters), a range of Bible study aids *and* abstracts of 70,000 articles from 300 religious and theological journals.

With a programme supplied by the firm that markets this disk (and, of course, the necessary hardware), you can type "r/john003:016" on your keyboard and nine versions of John 3:16 will flash on your computer screen at once.

The programme will also allow you to search instantly through any or all of those versions for a word or phrase you have in mind.

About the same time, I read a news story from the United Bible

Societies. It reported that Batak:Karo (Indonesia), chiTonga (Malawi), ekeGusii (Kenya), otjiHerero and ruKwangali (Namibia), Quechua:CUzco (Peru) and Tigre (Ethiopia) are the seven languages in which the first translation of the whole Bible appeared in 1988.

That brings to 310 the number of languages in which both the Old and New Testaments have been translated. The entire New Testament is available in another 695; and there are 1907 languages into which at least one book of the Bible has been translated.

It is no new insight that technological advances serve largely to increase the gap between those who have and those who have not.

What does it mean, though, when the technology gap manifests itself with respect to the scriptures?

The aims of those who offer computerized aids for biblical research are laudable. Who could argue against automating "the least productive and most tiring part" of Bible study — leafing through the pages? And, it will be pointed out, the technology already exists: why limit its use to those whose intentions are far less benign than students of the Bible?

Yet nagging doubts remain. Is the Word still a two-edged sword when it has become a string of characters that can be found electronically?

And is the Christian who "searches the scriptures" by loading it into a personal computer and pressing a few keys really doing the same thing as the Christian paging through a newly printed chiTonga Bible? Will they find the same light on life? If they find something different will they be able to share it with each other?

Typing these questions at my own computer, I have no answers. It is tempting to take refuge in scepticism: to argue that the maximum a computer can do is reduce drudgery and that those who discover really new insights from the biblical text on the screen would have found them anyway by using the old method.

Yet the thought won't quite go away that anything which widens the gap between a Christian in Canada and one in Malawi is something to lament.

June 1989

THE FRONT PAGE

When a political leader blurts out an off-the-cuff remark that diverges from the official line of his own party, or when events call into question some axiom of his worldview, a new sort of public relations expert is now available: the "spin doctor".

The image is derived from the billiards table. Depending on how and where you strike it, a cue ball will spin in different ways. How it spins determines where on the table it ends up after striking another ball.

At the billiards table, those gifted at imparting spin can perform feats which seem impossible to the ordinary bystander. A "spin doctor" who finds enough gullible ordinary bystanders — in a bar, for example — can earn a tidy (if disreputable) cash supplement to his or her income.

Metaphorically, a "spin doctor" is a specialist in a certain kind of interpretation — one which highlights what you like and plays down or disregards what you don't like, or one which accents an event's coherence with your beliefs while ignoring ways in which it might contradict them.

"Spin" may have been what one US journalist was asking for during the closing press conference at the WCC's world mission and evangelism meeting in San Antonio.

Midway through a marathon of plenary sessions in which a bewildering array of affirmations and appeals on a vast panoply of subjects was being articulated by a diverse range of people, this journalist understandably wondered how to explain to readers of a daily newspaper what was going on.

The difficulty she and her colleagues were experiencing may shed light on a question one local visitor to the conference posed to me: why isn't this story being covered on the front page of our local newspapers?

Isn't the sharing of experiences and insights going on here, she asked, at least as important as what *is* on the front page — the heat wave searing south Texas, the resignation of the speaker of the US House of Representatives, the inauguration of San Antonio's new mayor?

Ecumenical veterans could identify with the perplexity of a journalist trying for a succinct summary of San Antonio. Some expressed concern that if "mission in Christ's way" encompasses every item on the church's agenda, it blurs the focus on what many Christians understand by "mission".

In a sense, the "Message" adopted at San Antonio points to the heart of the problem: "the two most significant trends of this conference were the spirit of universality of the gathering and its concern for the fullness of the gospel", which requires holding "in creative tension spiritual and material needs, prayer and action, evangelism and social responsibility, dialogue and witness, power and vulnerability, local and universal".

"Creative tension" is, of course, a term that flows easily from the ecumenical pen. We are sometimes tempted to overlook the fact that even at its best "creative tension" is not only creative but also tense.

Maybe the tension in San Antonio — over how to articulate the mandate of mission alongside the mandate for dialogue or over how to issue a simultaneous call for proclamation and social engagement, without coining slogans or specifying shibboleths — didn't create enough conflict to attract the attention of those who decide what stories make it to the front page.

Be that as it may, San Antonio made the complexity of the mission agenda evident.

In the months to come, some may try to give this or that "spin" to their account of San Antonio. Far more important is how the churches, by themselves and together, come to terms with the myriad of challenges it has made clear.

July 1989

BUILDING TO THE GLORY OF GOD?

During one of my terms on the council of a small inner-city church it became clear that our wooden-frame chapel would no longer accommodate the number of Sunday-morning worshippers.

This led inexorably to the appointment of a committee. I've forgotten what name we gave it, but I recall that the suggestion "Building Committee" was ruled out at the start.

In part that was because we already had a Building Committee, made up of members who not only actually enjoyed plumbing and re-wiring but also had well-stocked personal tool kits.

More to the point, some people argued that putting the question of adequate worship space into the hands of a committee with the word "building" in its name was prejudging the case in favour of "bricks and mortar".

A number of socially committed members already had their eye on the abandoned showroom of an automobile dealer who had recently followed his prospective customers to the suburbs.

A certain polarization developed between those who favoured the "store-front church" model and those who maintained that a more responsible, if expensive, course of action was to witness to our commitment to the neighbourhood by constructing an attractive building.

You can imagine how the prooftexts lined up.

On the one side were those who pointed out that Stephen, shortly before his sermon was cut short by the lynch mob, reminded his listeners that "the Most High does not dwell in houses made with hands".

On the other side were those who recalled that Jesus said it was "a beautiful thing" when a woman poured expensive oil on his head and rebuked the disciples who argued that the amount of money it cost might better have been donated to the poor.

Building a place to worship God is always an ambiguous exercise.

Dwarfing the many other construction projects in Casablanca is the site of the Hassan II mosque. At the edge of the Atlantic Ocean stands the massive concrete shell of the building in the shadow of a 200-metre minaret.

Inside its vast expanse, a crew of 1500 is at work, welding, climbing scaffolds to position marble or cedar facades on walls and doors, preparing large underground bathing areas, painstakingly chipping elaborate geometric designs into pillars.

When the mosque is opened — in two years, it's hoped — it will hold 80,000 worshippers, the largest mosque in the world outside of Mecca.

An intensive solicitation drive, both within and outside the country, has so far collected the equivalent of something in the neighbourhood of US$500 million to defray construction costs.

Less than a generation after its independence from France, Morocco is not a wealthy country. Its population is growing rapidly, guaranteeing further strains on its economy.

The heritage of colonialism means that "the situation in which we are living we are not responsible for, and we have to re-establish Islam in Morocco", says University of Rabat Professor Abdessalam Boumijdid.

At the same time, there is pressure from other parts of the Muslim world to establish a certain kind of Islam. That message finds a ready hearing among the growing throngs of young people who, he said, "have no jobs and no goals".

For incurable editorialists, the Casablanca mosque raises on a grand scale the same issue our congregation faced: might this money have been better spent? But I wonder whether there aren't some prior questions one ought to pose to oneself. For a start, might this building in fact be to the glory of God? If I think so, how important is that? And if I don't think so, why not?

August/September 1989

FOOTNOTES AND PHOTOCOPIERS

My first encounter with plagiarism was in primary school, when a classmate made an oral report. Assigned to inform the class about some subject "in his own words", he made the encyclopedia's words his own by copying them in his own handwriting on a sheet of his own paper.

Alas, he did this so mechanically that he failed to omit the encyclopedia article's frequent parenthetical references to other entries. When he read his paper out, several incoherent phrases beginning with "see also . . ." marred what was otherwise an exceptionally articulate presentation for a ten-year-old.

Here was an unusually clear-cut illustration of the risks of plagiarism. Unlike many ordinary thefts, which may be disguised by reselling the pilfered goods or spending the stolen cash, the evidence of plagiarism endures, often in multiple copies, waiting to be discovered.

I recalled this inept misdemeanour when I read an *Ecumenical Press Service* dispatch headlined "Not Attributing Material Called Problem in Church".

Its occasion was a flurry of recent cases in which pastors-turned-authors have reproduced substantial chunks of material from someone else's book without informing readers of its source.

Only one of the three pastors cited in the story conceded that he should have acknowledged his source. Another insisted that he had never read the book from which he was alleged to have taken material. The third said the issue of giving credit had never crossed his mind.

A seminary professor quoted in the story suggested that pastors are bombarded with so many ideas from so many different sources that "they honestly don't know where they got the ideas to begin with".

Moreover, one might argue in mitigation, our conventions about things like footnotes are hardly rooted in eternal moral laws. After all, there are passages repeated almost word-for-word in several parts of the Old and New Testaments, without any indication of source.

Protecting "intellectual property" (the term also covers comic books and disco music) raises tricky moral and legal questions. Increasingly, these come to the fore in a world where information is power and the economic value of a computer programme or scientific formula may far exceed that of a steel mill.

Even before questions arose about the justice issues involved in allowing a person or company to "own" biotechnological secrets that may save lives or increase food production, it was recognized that knowledge advances by building on earlier knowledge. The ownership of ideas cannot be absolute.

But if we should not rush to judge people of plagiarism (imagine how footnotes in a sermon would dampen its kerygmatic punch!), we should perhaps acknowledge a certain insensitivity in this area among church people.

The photocopy machine has of course aggravated things. Choir directors who would never dream of padding an expense account or stealing a towel from a hotel room blithely disregard notices on sheet music forbidding unauthorized photocopying. It is doubtful that they do so as a conscientious act of civil disobedience against an unjust law.

October 1989

EXPERT UNEASE

For the past five years, the articles for each issue of *One World* have been typed into a computer in our office. After being sprinkled with a few simple codes that specify the format of the text, they are transmitted by telephone to our printer in Montreux whose computer converts them into the typeset form in which they eventually appear on our pages.

While understanding almost nothing about how this all works, I've become accustomed to the technological routine. From the point of view of time saved, the Wang is an unquestioned improvement on the balky Remington I inherited from my predecessors (to whom, I sometimes suspected, it may have been bequeathed by the Edinburgh world mission conference of 1910).

In some ways, I've made my peace with computers. To be sure, in an occasional moment of whimsical philosophizing, I may be tempted to grumble about what computers have done to our vocabulary. "Hardware", for instance, seems like the right word for those sturdy items forged of steel and wood which carpenters deploy, not for the delicate and bewildering complex of plastic and microchips that sits next to my desk.

"Capturing keystrokes" seems a doubtful improvement on "typing". "User-friendly" strikes me as an artificial attempt to introduce the illusion of personality into the "interface" between human and machine; moreover, some of the messages the computer sends — "Illegal width", it says if you inadvertently ask for a line with too many letters — betray a user-*unfriendly* smallness of spirit (Will I be penalized? Should I ask for forgiveness?).

Very recently we had our first serious problem with the system.

For reasons unknown (and perhaps unknowable), the texts for this issue became blocked, not once but twice. As their appearance in these pages suggests, we didn't actually lose them; but the original editing had to be redone and then redone again.

The whole business cost us perhaps a day and a half. As computer problems go, it was a minor one, not to be compared with, say, an airline reservations system or the stock exchange or the national defence computer going down. As general human problems go, it is hardly even worth mentioning.

But it does reveal our increasing dependence, in a technological age, on experts.

It's one thing to feel like Job (or Sisyphus) when a computer default that is beyond your technical grasp obliges you to redo and redo what you've already done. At the end of the day, that's just one more corollary of the dreary truth known to any car-owner: the more convenient the model, the less chance you'll be able to do anything at all about problems that arise.

Far more serious is the realization that so central an issue for our common future as making decisions about developing weapons is beyond the grasp not only of ordinary people who would like to assess it ethically but also of the very government officials charged with the deciding.

As the director of a UK research group on militarism, Scilla Elworthy, warns, there is a further risk. If you try to rectify this situation and learn a lot about modern weapons, chances are you will be co-opted into accepting the premisses of those who develop them.

At the same time, describing weapons development in terms of "technological push" — an inexorable process that runs under its own steam — might be a vivid metaphor to correct our easy optimism, but it obscures the reality that it is in fact people, with distinct interests of their own, who do the pushing.

One wonders whether those of us in the church, hearing our moral pronouncements about war and peace ruled irrelevant because we don't understand the technology, dare to ask ourselves how often we cloak our own message in terms too arcane for most people to bother with?

January/February 1990

THE TIMES THEY ARE A-CHANGIN'

Change and decay in all around I see:
O Thou who changest not, abide with me.

Pleading for the security of the presence of a faithful God, these lines from a familiar 19th-century hymn imply a rather negative view of change, pairing it with decay. Change illustrates the precariousness of life and shakes the fragile confidence we manage to build on the status quo.

In support of the suspicion that change is usually for the worse, life throws up an almost infinite range of evidence: often trifling (why does the mass-produced tomato taste so awful?), sometimes questionable (why aren't there any great preachers anymore?), occasionally terrifying (remember when avarice was thought to be something shameful?). Especially as we grow older, such changes fuel nostalgia for "golden ages" and "good old days".

Unnerved by change, we may be less sensitive to the deadliness of the outlooks on life which often accompany commitment to the status quo: smug self-satisfaction for some, complacency for many others, resignation for most.

Recent months have brought great changes to Eastern Europe. Political upheaval and talk of economic change present churches there with new opportunities and responsibilities and challenge churches elsewhere to seek appropriate responses.

The exhilaration of these changes may leave us breathless, susceptible to several temptations.

A few will be tempted to euphoria. The most lavish form this has taken under the present circumstances is the "end of history" thesis: the suggestion that the events in Eastern Europe signal the end not just of cold war ideological conflict, but of human ideological evolution, with the universalization of Western liberal democracy. Others may be tempted in the opposite direction — to the cynicism of refusing to believe that anything ever really changes.

In the face of these changes, some will find it irresistible to say "I told you so". Others, recognizing the passing of realities long taken for granted and thus of familiar ways of dealing with those realities, are eager to find new certainties. Yet if the changes show us that we have seen "through a glass darkly" in the past, do they not also hint that we may go on seeing through a glass darkly?

Is it not best for Christians outside Eastern Europe to give acts of solidarity with the churches there (in the first place, prayer) priority over attempts to speak a definitive or prophetic word? Perhaps it is good to practise the discipline of listening silently to the voices of often-silenced fellow Christians. (This will be complicated, of course, by the fact that they will not necessarily be speaking with one voice.)

The size and scale of the changes in Eastern Europe may tempt us to the self-deception of what John Yoder once called "the lunge for the large view". By many criteria, he argues, "who is in high office or what laws are written will make less difference" twenty years hence "than the cumulation of an infinity of tiny deeds: mothers who feed their children, children who learn their lessons, craftsmen who finish a job, doctors who get the dosage right, drivers who stay on the road, policemen who hold their fire".

Fascination with the spectacular changes wrought by revolution may lead us to undervalue slower and less visible changes — the "infinity of tiny deeds" that constitute seeds of hope or signs of decay.

Christians who hear a call to be agents of change run up against a humbling biblical image — the little yeast that leavens a whole loaf. At the same time, they recall that the one who used that image has promised to be with us always, whatever the changes.

March 1990

MAKE ME AN INSTRUMENT

Among the best-loved Christian prayers is the one attributed to St Francis of Assisi which begins "Lord, make me an instrument of your peace. . . ."

The combination of submissiveness and action in this familiar prayer inspires and challenges Christians to dare to be used by God. At its root is a profound paradox of Christian existence: that our freedom is most fully realized in binding ourselves to God's will — for, as the last line of the prayer says, "it is in dying that we are born to eternal life".

The idea of being an instrument is not always accompanied by such lofty sentiments. For some, the plea to "make me an instrument" seems to come with the unspoken proviso: "so long as it isn't second fiddle".

The word "instrument" is often use ecumenically for the various organizational manifestations of the movement for or vision of Christian unity. An *instrument* of the ecumenical movement is an institution seeking to keep alive and advance the goals of the movement. As these aims evolve and the context in which one strives for them changes, the instrument must develop.

Ay, there's the rub, as Shakespeare would put it. When an instrument takes institutional form, adapting to new vision or new realities is complicated by a range of pressures that individuals do not face.

Articles in this issue describe how some ecumenical instruments are seeking to adapt these days. At its eighth assembly, a new vision of the Lutheran World Federation (LWF) was inextricably tied to questions of restructuring. The challenge of redefining a role and a vision in a totally altered situation of Eastern Europe faces the Christian Peace Conference.

The fifth assembly of the Middle East Council of Churches (MECC), which saw the formal entry of Roman Catholic Middle East churches into its membership, has been described as a watershed, marking a new era for the churches — and their ecumenical instrument — in the area where Christianity was born and first divided. That means anything but "business as usual".

Whether carefully planned for 1992 or unforeseen and happening every day, changes in Europe mean churches there must find new ways to be an instrument of justice, peace and the integrity of creation.

Each of our stories makes it clear that the imperative of producing a better ecumenical instrument is linked with financial constraints. The LWF budget is to be cut and its staff reduced; CPC income may be diminished as its main source, the Moscow Patriarchate, faces new opportunities in its own setting; more financial support from within the region has been described as an "acid test" for the MECC; ecumenical bodies dealing with European questions are chronically underfunded.

(It's difficult not to feel a certain bitterness about that when reading that a Wall Street firm, one of whose brokers earned US$500 million in a recent year, paid some of its employees Christmas bonuses up to $10 million — and then declared bankruptcy in February.)

Other sorts of bitterness come when ecumenical instruments face the reality of adjusting and adapting and cutting. The pain of that process is not necessarily soothed by hopes that a better instrument will result. For those feeling such pain, the most difficult petition of St Francis's prayer is probably: "Grant that we may not so much seek to be consoled as to console, to be understood as to understand. . . ."

April 1990

INTERCONNECTEDNESSES

The not-particularly-melodious word "interconnectedness" comes up often in discussion of justice, peace and the integrity of creation — subject of the WCC's 1990 world convocation on JPIC in Seoul, Korea.

As many as seven types of interconnectedness emerge from the JPIC process. (There may be more, but having got to seven, one is tempted to stop counting.)

First and fundamental is the interconnectedness of justice, peace and the integrity of creation. Ecumenical discussions have identified the international debt crisis as perhaps the clearest example of this linkage.

Justice is threatened in the most debt-burdened countries because the economic situation takes its heaviest toll on the weakest, especially women and children. Peace is at risk because military force may be needed to back up unpopular measures imposed by international financial powers. Generating exports to repay the debt often threatens fragile ecosystems, for example through deforestation or cash-cropping on marginal land.

Creation itself reveals a second type of interconnectedness, echoed in the phrase "integrity of creation". In a sermon in Seoul WCC president Marga Bührig from Switzerland observed that Psalm 104's vivid language about creation portrays "a great fabric in which everything is interwoven, all things living depend on God . . . and live in company with each other".

A third kind of interconnectedness is that which links the struggles of people in different parts of the world against the forces of death.

This is more than a sentimental recognition that "no one is an island", that anyone's suffering affects everyone. It results from the interconnectedness of the forces of death that oppress people around the world.

Yet the danger is always present, Philippine Roman Catholic theologian and activist Ed de la Torre observed in Seoul, that those whose struggle ought to bring them into solidarity with each other instead fall into the trap of asking, "but why isn't *my* pain being mentioned?"

Related to this is a fourth interconnectedness: the link between the global and the local. This led to some tensions in Seoul, with many people charging that speaking globally is an exercise in abstraction that is remote from and irrelevant to real-life, day-to-day struggle.

A fifth interconnectedness applies particularly to the ecumenical movement: the link — and corresponding tension — between "unity" or "Faith and Order" concerns (the ideal of JPIC as a "conciliar process") and "mission" or "Life and Work" concerns (what the churches *do* for justice, peace and creation).

Stated differently, this is the tension between "theology" and "ethics", an issue the WCC's first general secretary W. A. Visser 't Hooft addressed (but did not lay to rest) in his oft-quoted remark that "church members who deny in fact their responsibility for the needy . . . are just as much guilty of heresy as those who deny this or that article of the faith".

A sixth interconnectedness brought out by the JPIC process is that between "social" ethics and "personal" ethics. This link asks us to consider what this one struggle for justice, peace and for the integrity of creation may require of us as individuals.

Might it demand a change of personal lifestyle — even if it is clear that *my* giving up spray deodorant or grain-fed beef or a private car will make only an infinitesimal difference to the ozone layer or world hunger or the "greenhouse effect"?

Finally, there is the interconnectedness of what has already been said and done in the ecumenical movement with what is being said and done today.

"Grant us wisdom, grant us courage . . .", participants sang during a worship service in Seoul. It is not always easy — especially for those new to the ecumenical fellowship — to see that achieving wisdom may involve building on earlier insights, even though new challenges demand new responses.

Yet is it not this interconnectedness that keeps the ecumenical movement moving?

May 1990

MY AUTO, RIGHT OR WRONG?

According to what has been called "the law of unintended consequences", well-meant changes for the better almost inevitably make some things worse.

For example, some argue, opening a wider variety of jobs to women has had the unintended consequence of lowering the overall quality of elementary education. When becoming a primary schoolteacher was one of few career options for educated women, far more talented women were drawn to elementary classrooms than today, when all sorts of other professions beckon.

An unintended consequence of the opening of the Berlin Wall, said a report on the BBC recently, has been a marked increase in traffic fatalities in East Germany — nearly 50 percent higher during the first three months of 1990 than in the same period last year.

A third of the accidents, statistics say, involved cars registered in West Germany. As causes for the surge in traffic deaths, accident investigators singled out excessive speed (East German motorways have a speed limit of 100 kilometres an hour, West German ones have none), drinking, unfamiliarity with signposting and poor road conditions. Nevertheless, according to the BBC, the West German transport minister says the Federal Republic's traffic code will apply in a reunited Germany.

All this set me to wondering about the relative rarity of the automobile as a topic of moral discourse. During the Vietnam War, opponents of the antiwar movement sometimes complained about the "selective morality" of protestors who mourned the hundreds of US troops killed but said not a word about the far greater number of people dying on US highways.

At the time, that argument struck me as a perverse distraction from the real issue. It still seems ethically irrelevant: neither supporters nor opponents of the Vietnam War ought to have been measuring its morality by the number of US soldiers killed. But why are we so reluctant to think about traffic deaths (except perhaps those caused by drunken driving) in terms of good and evil, right and wrong?

I suspect it is because in many parts of the world the automobile is so all-pervasive — not only as an economic reality, but also as a cultural artifact and a political symbol of individual freedom — that life without it is unimaginable and moral discourse about it thus seems bound in a straitjacket. The devastation wrought by the automobile seems no more susceptible to ethical reflection than that caused by floods or tornadoes.

Let me be honest. I suspect my own changing attitudes about the automobile are less a product of refined ethical sensitivity than of growing resentment — over time wasted in traffic jams along Geneva's clogged arteries, over the aggressive discourtesy of drivers who seek an advantage in those situations by cutting in front of me, over the substantial part of my monthly income that hemorrhages away in license fees, insurance, fuel and maintenance. Yet though living with my car may be no picnic, the prospect of living without it requires more energy or creativity than I've yet mustered.

Today, of course, we are coming to an increasing recognition that the unrestrained production and deployment of automobiles may not only raise uncomfortable questions about our obedience to the commandment "Thou shalt not kill". It may also have incalculable ecological consequences.

Even here, we hesitate morally. Is it really true, I wonder, that my ageing, rust-scarred Peugeot has, since 1983, annually released its own weight in carbon dioxide into the atmosphere, thus doing its part for global warming through the "greenhouse effect"? Moreover, if the scientists prove to my satisfaction that this is the case, what should I do about it? Do I really need to wait until ethicists and preachers tell me?

June 1990

109

ANGER

Reading New Zealand Associated Churches of Christ minister Ron O'Grady's article on child prostitution in Asia made me angry.

On reflection, I was struck by how seldom I would use the word "anger" to describe my reaction to what I read in *One World*. And that made me wonder what it was about this article that made me angry and why am I not angry more often.

The first question is the easier one. The enslavement of children and their vulnerability to this kind of slavery takes an added emotional force when one reads, as a parent of teen-age daughters, about Aw, an "old woman" at 13.

The rage is only heightened by the thought of the well-to-do foreigners for whom this slave trade exists bringing video cameras to record their own degradation and produce their own private pornography.

But if the anger was easy to explain, the second question — why I am not angry more often — was not. It became particularly pointed when I reread Indian Roman Catholic theologian Samuel Rayan's litany of what grieves the Holy Spirit. About these realities of today, Rayan says, "God weeps, his Christ sheds tears and his Spirit grieves and sighs". And we don't often even get angry.

Anger, said the 17th-century essayist Thomas Fuller, "is one of the sinews of the soul". Does our failure to react angrily to what we know about hundreds of situations in the world today indicate spiritual flabbiness? Or is it just a matter of numbness?

Perhaps testimonies of suffering too often come to us in abstract and general terms, already packaged as a "problem" or a "crisis" or an "issue", for which we may work and hope and pray that a solution will be found, but to which we do not attach a human face.

110

Perhaps our notion of evil is so determined by the intellectual recognition of the sin embedded in social structures that we have forgotten about sinners. Only when a massive social catastrophe like child prostitution is exemplified for us in an individual story does it hit us in a way that elicits anger.

But if our lack of anger raises questions about our spiritual health, several New Testament passages seem to suggest that anger, too, is hazardous for the well-being of our souls.

Jesus utters a particularly ominous warning about anger in the Sermon on the Mount (Matthew 5:21-24). He extends the Old Testament prohibition of murder to the anger which often lies behind it.

A well-known passage in the letter to the Ephesians (4:26) seems somewhat more permissive: "Be angry but do not sin; do not let the sun go down on your anger." But sinless anger may be a counsel of perfection beyond the reach of most of us, and in any case the apostle calls on his readers a few verses later to put away anger.

From the context of these two passages, it appears that what is being condemned is the anger of personal insults and vendettas which eat away at the community of believers.

Another New Testament passage (admittedly written before psychologists discovered the value of venting your feelings and the danger of repressing them) offers a perhaps more pertinent warning: "Let everyone be quick to hear, slow to speak, slow to anger, for human anger does not work the righteousness of God" (James 1:19-20).

Can these texts be a guide for dealing with our anger about child prostitution? Is the point that we should not let the sun go down on that rage, but ought to be about the humble search for a way in which our anger can be converted into something that can "work the righteousness of God"?

Of course, it is far more likely that our anger about child prostitution will have disappeared the next morning because we have forgotten about it, added it to the long list of things about which we no longer get angry.

July 1990

LOVE AND HATE

Does the ecumenical movement help us to *love* better?

That question struck me as unusual when the veteran Roman Catholic ecumenist Tom Stransky posed it during a recent conversation about how churches see the ecumenical movement, the WCC, themselves and each other.

Stransky called for an ecumenism that is not only "catalytic", arousing divided Christians to live up to their confession of "one holy catholic church", but also "therapeutic", providing an antidote to the widespread misuse of religion to justify our sicknesses. "Helping us to love better" is one way to describe this dimension of ecumenism.

During the same week as this conversation took place, a group of what *The New York Times* called "luminaries" met in Oslo to discuss "The Anatomy of Hate — Resolving Conflict through Dialogue and Democracy". The roster of participants ranged from Nelson Mandela, François Mitterand and Václav Havel to Salvadorean Lutheran Bishop Medardo Gomez and Lutheran World Federation general secretary Gunnar Staalsett.

Nobel prizewinning author Elie Wiesel, a survivor of the Holocaust, said the conference was urgent at this time because "ethnic, religious and national hatreds are re-emerging with a vengeance".

A closing "Oslo Declaration" called hatred an "ancient scourge, whose origins remain hidden in darkness; . . . a black sun which, from under an ashen sky, hits and kills all those who forget the greatness of which they are capable and the promises once bestowed on them".

Hatred is "the negation of every triumph that culture and civilization may achieve. . . . Religious hatred makes the face of God invisible. Political hatred wipes out people's liberties. In the field of Science, ha-

112

tred inevitably puts itself at Death's service. In Literature, it distorts Truth, perverts the meaning of the story and hides Beauty itself under a thick layer of blood and grime."

The *Times* detected differences among participants over how their theme related to the Gulf crisis.

Jimmy Carter doubted that "democracy" is an answer to hate, charging that Western democracies often personalize hatred — as when they add Iraqi President Saddam Hussein to the list of enemies "stripped of any redeeming human characteristics". On the other hand, argued Irish writer Conor Cruise O'Brien, "Dialogue alone is not going to get Saddam Hussein out of Kuwait."

German writer Günter Grass, attacking firms in his country that sold arms to Iraq, spoke of uncontrolled lust for profits, rather than hate, as a motivating force behind the crisis. Norwegian foreign minister Kjell Bondevik saw in the Gulf situation "a tragic reminder" that "we have done far too little to eradicate the conditions under which hate flourishes".

"To hate is to opt for the easiest and most mind-reducing way out," says the Oslo Declaration. Those who hate look at others — and at themselves — "not as a subject of pride but as an object of disdain and fear".

Some may argue that the complexities of the Gulf crisis prove that to zero in on hatred, as the Oslo conference did, is also a kind of opting for an "easy way out". They may be tempted to agree with Yelena Bonner, Andrej Sakharov's widow, that "a lot of the talk here is just meaningless platitudes". Others may have theological reservations about such assertions as "because hatred is willed by Man, God himself is unable to stop it" but "humanity is strong enough to stem it".

Yet do we not risk missing something essential when we skip over simple ideas like love and hate — when we go straight to the ambiguities and complexities and theological reservations, bypassing the horrifying mystery of hate when we describe the state of the world, overlooking the breathtaking challenge of *loving better* when we explain why we care about the ecumenical movement?

October 1990

PASSIONATE CERTAINTY

Accepting the legitimacy of plurality is difficult for those who are "passionately certain" about things, Philippine Roman Catholic theologian and activist Ed de la Torre suggested at the recent World Student Christian Federation assembly. One need not search very far to find examples of the hatred and bloodshed that passionate certainty can create.

Some are passionately certain about the promise of a new Jewish temple in Jerusalem. Others, devout Muslims, revere this site as one of Islam's holiest places. When these two passionate convictions encountered each other last month, twenty-one Palestinians lost their lives.

Passionate certainty is deaf to voices like those of the participants in the recent multi-faith consultation sponsored by the WCC in Hong Kong. They called for an affirmation of plurality and the building up of a "culture of dialogue", beginning at the local level.

The evil created by passionate certainties — from name-calling and stereotyping to crusades and pogroms — may tempt us to glorify uncommitted agnosticism. With all the pain inflicted by those who harbour no doubts about the rightness of their belief and the justice of their cause, might it not be better to remain detached, dispassionate, not quite convinced?

Many challenge that sort of shrinking back from passionate certainty. A group of people meet in Hong Kong to learn together ecumenically about evangelism. From widely different backgrounds, they join to speak with passionate certainty: "Re-ignited by the love of Jesus Christ . . . and by the greatness of the gospel in every culture, we are burning to proclaim the wonders of God!"

Many black Christians in US cities live amidst seemingly endless violence and misery created by intractable social injustice. Yet their churches are "islands of warmth and caring and love", where worship is "filled with joy and a living faith". Could that happen without a passionate certainty about the gospel of Jesus Christ and the way of life it calls us to?

The participants in the Hong Kong meeting did not believe that passionate certainty and acceptance of pluralism are mutually exclusive — no matter how difficult it is to hold the two together. They appealed for passionate certainty ("speaking the truth as we see it" and "acting upon the basic commitments of our faith") to be expressed within a pluralistic context ("in our own life situations").

They did not say this in naïve or idealistic ignorance of the tensions between Jews and Muslims. Indeed, some of the pain that has scarred relations between these two peoples surfaced explicitly in Hong Kong.

A clue to the sort of passionate certainty that is called for comes from Stephen Larson's reflections on liturgy and social justice. Larson is pastor of the English-speaking Lutheran congregation in Geneva.

In the "unambiguous" proclamation of God's word in worship, there is a passionate certainty that denounces "the world's bad news" of "injustice, oppression, the exploitation of the created order" and "condemns those who pretend to serve God and wealth". But another unambiguous certainty is also proclaimed: "the prodigal nature of God's grace, God's longing to love, forgive, comfort and uphold the people of God".

Paul Crow, president of the Council on Christian Unity of the Christian Church (Disciples of Christ) in the US and Canada, speaks of another passionate commitment — that of the saints, who understood that "renewal comes to those whose obedience to God leads them to the cross" and were willing to be obedient even unto death.

Perhaps one of the biggest problems facing the church and the ecumenical movement today, Crow suggests, is that "we do not believe that the renewal for which our world is yearning comes only as self-assertion gives way to self-denial."

God's grace and our call to self-denial — here are certainties about which one can be passionate and pluralistic.

November 1990

115

THE INNOCENTS

One episode comes immediately to mind if we seek analogies between the story of the Christ-child and the children for whose welfare world leaders solemnly pledged their concern at the recent UN-sponsored World Summit for Children.

It is Herod's gruesome killing of babies in the region of Bethlehem and the resulting period of uncertainty for the Holy Family — first as refugees in Egypt, then as repatriated exiles settling in Galilee rather than Judaea out of fear of Herod's son Archelaus, the new king (Matthew 2:22-23).

Despite the precarious situation of his family, we are told by another gospel-writer, "the child grew and became strong, filled with wisdom; and the favour of God was upon him" (Luke 2:40).

In short, we know little about Jesus the child, except that after a period of danger he not only survived but thrived. The ecumenical creeds leap quickly from Jesus' miraculous birth to his suffering and crucifixion "under Pontius Pilate".

Perhaps this silence is just as well. Some early Christians, unsatisfied with the spare accounts of the canonical gospels, did invent supplementary stories of the young Jesus as a prodigious miracle-worker. No doubt they did so out of piety as well as curiosity, but "the Jesus who is thus portrayed," notes Edwin Yamauchi in the *International Standard Bible Encyclopaedia*, "appears as a grotesquely petulant and dangerously powerful youngster".

The fate of the "holy innocents" slaughtered by the paranoid Herod in a horrifyingly unsuccessful effort to protect his crown, and commemorated by many church traditions on 28 December, seems to offer a closer parallel to the fate of millions of children in the world today.

116

Telling this story, the writer of the gospel of Matthew recalled a passage in Jeremiah: "A voice was heard in Ramah, weeping and loud lamentation, Rachel weeping for her children; she refused to be consoled, because they are no more" (Matthew 2:18).

For "Ramah", we may read "Juba" or "Cairo" or "Calcutta" or "São Paulo" or "the South Bronx" — or any of a thousand other places where mothers weep for children who "are no more".

We should be mindful of two misunderstandings in making this comparison. In the first place, despite the conventional use of the term "holy innocents" (going back at least to the third century), it was neither these children's moral blamelessness nor their irrelevance to the political machinations of first-century Judaea that made Herod's act evil. The rights of children, above all to life in all its fullness, do not derive from their goodness or their vulnerability, but from their creation in the image of God.

Second, such savagery as Herod's action illustrates accounts for only a tiny portion of the deaths of children. The world leaders gathered in New York at the summit acknowledged this. Many of those deaths could be prevented by relatively simple and inexpensive measures — if, as the Canadian prime minister pointed out, there were "the political will" to re-order priorities.

In this, as in many other contexts, "political will" can be a massive abstraction, allowing us to disperse blame so widely through the system that it never even occurs to us to imagine ourselves in Herod's camp when it comes to the suffering and death of children.

But the reminder of the need for "political will" can also be a challenge to churches and Christians to accept the opportunities they have to shape the ordering of priorities in their own societies and the world as a whole.

December 1990

EXERCISING CHRISTIANITY

The well-publicized visit by US President George Bush to military forces in Saudi Arabia coincided with the country's annual Thanksgiving Day holiday.

The usual centrepiece of this celebration (whose origins go back to the Pilgrims' gratitude for having survived the rigours of their first year in North America) is a sumptuous dinner of roast turkey and an array of trimmings.

In 1990, more than 200,000 US servicemen and women stationed in the Gulf could not be with loved ones on Thanksgiving — traditionally the family holiday *par excellence*.

But no effort was spared in seeking to boost their morale by airlifting to the desert vast quantities of typical holiday fare — a one-day respite from the dreariness of field rations and bottled water turned hot under the Saudi sun.

What this celebration did *not* involve, in Saudi Arabia at least, was any allusion by the president to the action from which the holiday derives its name: grateful prayer to God for blessings symbolized by the bountiful spread.

The reason for Mr Bush's reticence, according to a *New York Times* story, was a firm intention not to offend the Muslims of Saudi Arabia, where organized religions other than Islam are prohibited. He did join in prayers with sailors on the *Nassau*, an amphibious assault vessel "in international waters".

Before Mr Bush's visit, a White House spokesperson, noting that "we have to spend a lot of time thinking about these things", put it this way: "There will be no presidential exercise of Christianity on Saudi soil."

This awkward officialese invites several immediate retorts. Some will voice the hope that Administration officials are spending even more time thinking about such things as how to resolve the crisis peacefully.

Some will insist that in fact the chief executive of a pluralistic country which makes separation of church and state an article of faith ought never to indulge in "presidential exercises of Christianity".

Others will observe that Thanksgiving Day prayers in any case tend to be more redolent of smug civil religion than of biblical Christianity, or that it's only for the best if Christianity doesn't get mixed up in military operations with code names like "Imminent Thunder", or that the feat of flying a quarter of a million turkey dinners halfway around the world while millions go hungry is a damning reflection of the world's priorities.

There is another pertinent issue lurking beneath the government official's words. "*No* presidential exercise of Christianity"?, one wants to ask.

Are we to suppose that Mr Bush passed his entire time "on Saudi soil" being careful not to evidence love for neighbour or compassion for the hurting, that he suppressed any silent prayer which might have come to his mind, that he was not sustained by any "assurance of things hoped for" or confidence in the promise that "my grace is sufficient for you"?

There is no way to answer these questions; and in a sense, of course, we have no business wondering in this way about the personal faith of the US president.

But the easy equation of the "exercise of Christianity" with public acts of piety should remind us anew of the situation of Christians in many countries for whom open worship and witness are blocked for reasons far more compelling than self-imposed restrictions on religious freedom for diplomatic purposes. The silence of their witness has not always been viewed sympathetically by Christians outside.

This also raises a more jarring question. Could it be that the fact that there are places where public "exercise of Christianity" is prohibited says as much about how Christianity has typically been exercised by "Christian" countries as it does about the countries that make such prohibitions?

January 1991

119

BEYOND TRIUMPHALISM

> *What though the spicy breezes*
> *Blow soft o'er Ceylon's isle;*
> *Though every prospect pleases,*
> *And only man is vile:*
> *In vain with lavish kindness*
> *The gifts of God are strown;*
> *The heathen in his blindness*
> *Bows down to wood and stone.*

Well-intended though it may have been, the missionary hymn ("From Greenland's Icy Mountains") of Bishop Reginald Heber (1783-1826) is often cited as uniquely illustrative of everything that was wrong with the worldwide expansion of Christian evangelization in the 19th century.

The bishop probably meant to celebrate the triumph of the gospel; instead, the song reveals the triumphalism of a church that did not trouble to make too fine a distinction between itself and expansionist Western civilization.

That sense is reinforced by the portrayal of mission as travelogue and of those to whom the word is to be preached as "heathens". (In fact, the *Oxford Dictionary of Quotations* notes, the author at this point toned down his original text, which spoke of "savages".)

It's been years since I recall singing the quaint-sounding lines of this song, long since expurgated from many hymnbooks and living on only in irreverent parodies. Yet the verse above crept back into my mind while I was reading about the agony of Sri Lanka.

Breezes over Sri Lanka today are more likely to waft the pungent odours of explosives and death than of the exotic spices Bishop Heber had in mind.

It is the seemingly endless cycle of terror and counter-terror (of which the strife in Sri Lanka is only a single and often unnoticed case), not the worship of "graven images", that illustrates most clearly the vileness of humanity in our time. And only those who are most resolutely blind to reality imagine that human vileness can be geographically localized.

Not so obvious, perhaps, is another inappropriateness of the sentiments of hymns like this one today. It is evident in the way the strife in places like Sri Lanka mocks our easy assumptions that we somehow have the answer.

Having heard often enough about the unsavoury alliance of gospel and colonialism, we may avoid the grosser versions of missionary triumphalism. But we must be wary of supposing that our more chastened messages of justice and reconciliation and common humanity need only to be properly heard if peace is to break out among warring parties in Sri Lanka — or anywhere else where hatreds old and new cause daily suffering and death. It's simply not that easy.

The danger with chastened triumphalism is that it may beget cynicism and despair. Having resisted the temptation to disregard the limitations on what we can do in cases like these, we may fall to the next temptation: that of classifying Sri Lanka among those situations in which the only hope is that someday exhaustion will end the conflict.

The report of an ecumenical team visit to Sri Lanka suggests an extraordinarily difficult mandate for churches around the world (though it's modest by comparison with the calling of the churches there): a prayerful solidarity with the people of Sri Lanka, ever conscious of the limits of our solidarity, unwaveringly convinced of the limitless possibilities of prayer.

February 1991

A CUP OF COFFEE

When the price of a 250-gramme package of coffee beans dropped to Sfr. 2.00 last week (the last time I checked, the same package cost Sfr. 3.70), I thought about buying a few extras to store in the freezer. In the end, I didn't: a malfunction in the cooling mechanism had temporarily put our refrigerator out of service.

Needless to say, the lower price of coffee beans has not induced any of the handful of restaurants with which I am acquainted to charge less for a cup of coffee. Though it's not clear to me exactly how these things get decided (perhaps the cost of hot water has shot up in the meantime), my impression is that if the price of coffee beans were to rise, it would be reflected — and rather quickly — in what one pays for a cup of coffee.

More to the point, I don't really understand why the price of coffee is suddenly so low. But Peter Crossman, general secretary of the European Ecumenical Organization for Development, argues that the countries who depend on selling coffee are not among those best placed to absorb loss of income. And it goes without saying that the poorest people in those countries are the ones who will suffer the most as a result.

The price of coffee reminds me that I buy a lot of produce and groceries at a price which is determined in ways I don't understand, though it seems to involve something more complicated than our old friend from elementary economics: the law of supply and demand.

It has been suggested that anyone who watched sausage being made would probably, on aesthetic grounds alone, never eat it again. Would understanding the process by which farm products, especially those from faraway countries, arrive on the supermarket shelf lead to similar opting out on ethical grounds?

I'm not enthusiastic about finding out, if the consequence is asking myself whether I should give up my morning cup or two of coffee — though I suppose I could manage that.

It's tempting to duck behind the argument that the structures which make it possible to buy coffee or cocoa or fresh oranges or bananas in countries where it is too cold to grow them are so vast and complicated that my opting out of the system would create scarcely a ripple.

Yet these are matters that touch rather directly on the fundamental human rights of people in developing countries. Depriving a country of "food security", Crossman says, is "morally unacceptable".

Two challenges, it seems to me, face the churches when they deplore the injustices that are built into global economic systems.

One is abstract and global: if this is injustice, what would justice look like?

The other is concrete and individual, but no less daunting: what guidance for my personal decision-making follows from this understanding of systemic injustice?

This is of course the issue of Christian life-style: the range of everyday choices one feels called upon to make in living out one's Christian commitment.

Fraught as it is with the risks of self-righteousness, legalism and absolutization of the habits of one's own culture, this is a subject which the churches ecumenically have been hesitant to enter into very explicitly.

"As churches draw closer to each other on the ecumenical pilgrimage," said the WCC's seventh assembly in Canberra, "they are increasingly recognizing the place of *Christian life-style,* spiritual discipline, holiness, a spirituality of active non-violence. . . .

"We therefore call on the World Council of Churches to explore the various forms and expressions of ecumenical spirituality. . . ."

What kind of guidance, I wonder, will such an exploration offer me as I push my shopping cart down the aisle of the supermarket?

May 1991

BARRIER-FREE?

Most highways out of Geneva lead directly into France. Before arriving though, one must pass a customs post.

Under normal circumstances this is routine, at least if you have a Geneva-registered car and no passengers who look to the border guard like asylum-seekers. A nod from the official, a simple slalom around the barrier, and the frontier is crossed.

Long ago, "at the east of Eden the Lord placed the cherubim, and a sword flaming and turning to guard the way to the tree of life" (Genesis 3:24). Ever since, boundaries and barriers have been a feature of human life.

Boundaries and barriers can be extraordinarily complicated. The complications are not just intellectual puzzles but factors affecting the lives of millions.

In the aftermath of the Gulf War (touched off when Iraq sought to erase the boundary between it and Kuwait), global attention has been drawn to the pain of the Kurdish people and, consequently, to their dispersion across five countries with no boundaries of their own.

As defined by international conventions, refugees are people who flee for their lives or safety across national boundaries. (Those who flee for their lives but do not cross frontiers present an even more difficult problem.)

The boundary between East and West Germany was marked by one of the most vivid symbols of the contemporary world — the Berlin Wall. Now it has been dismantled, and the boundary it symbolized is no more.

National frontiers are not the only barriers. Large barriers are set up by differing faith commitments — barriers that need more than simple goodwill to overcome.

When people with disabilities speak about barriers, they may mean something as mundane as a stairway or narrow aisle — or as profound as the attitudes which block Christians from seeing their difficulties and gifts.

One reason the World Council of Churches was formed, says its constitution, was "to express the common concerns of the churches in . . . breaking down barriers between people". It's an inspiring goal, echoing the apostle's description of what Christ's coming implied for Jews and non-Jews alike: "in his flesh he has made both groups into one and has broken down the dividing wall, that is, the hostility between us" (Ephesians 2:14). The very next words in the constitution speak of "the promotion of one human family in justice and peace" — a phrase that sounds a lot like the title of this magazine.

How do we understand this in a day when new barriers are being built and the absence of barriers often seems to create as many problems as it solves? "Good fences make good neighbors", a poet once wrote. But how do fences and other barriers function in "one human family", in "one world"?

June 1991

125

ELECTRONIC VOICES

In his novel *Brazzaville Beach*, William Boyd describes how the stability of a massive skyscraper depends on precise placement of bolts in the steel girders that form its superstructure. An error of a few millimetres in drilling a hole at ground level may yawn, eighty floors up, into a gap of several metres.

That image captures some initial misgivings I felt when reading the fascinating account by Alastair Hulbert of the Church of Scotland of "GulfWatch" — a computer conference network organized during the recent conflict by a Scottish ecumenical organization.

I speak as one as yet unbitten by the computer conferencing bug: sceptical but not (I hope) closed-minded, intrigued by the comparison drawn by British journalist Martin Walker (a recent recruit): it's like "attending a bizarre party where everyone is drunk enough to be frank, sober enough to be lucid".

Ignorance of the sources of the input into computer conferences heightens the usual question of how you know what to believe. When I encounter a news item on the Voice of America or in a release from the Middle East Council of Churches or in a conversation with my brother-in-law, my assessment of it is coloured by what (I believe) I know of the source. How does one gain a similar background when reading things on a computer screen? "The anonymity of the electrons" may "loosen inhibitions and spur ideas", as Walker says, but it doesn't do much for guaranteeing factuality and reliability.

An example Hulbert raises in this connection — "Three hundred thousand dead? Are the exact numbers as relevant as the fact of their dying?" — evokes familiar warning signals. "Well, yes, it does," one wants to argue. Doesn't exaggerating casualty statistics in the hope of

126

making war's horror clearer boil down to trying to serve the truth by falsehood? Is there anyone whose motives are demonstrably so pure that we would be willing to offer him or her the license to do that?

Moreover, if the inflated figure later proves significantly off the mark, doesn't it offer an easy way out to those who would prefer to ignore the horrors in the first place? Doesn't even a small mistake in ground-floor statistics destabilize the whole structure built on them?

It seems to me, on reflection, that this line of argument would be considerably more persuasive if the news professionals who told the ongoing story of the Gulf War had done a notably better job of keeping us informed. Committed to the highest standards of objective journalism and endowed with the latest technology, they managed to produce a running account that surely exceeded the fondest hopes of the military news managers. We learned a lot about "smart bombs", but no one told us until much later that 93 per cent of what the planes were dropping were of the old indiscriminate variety.

War, in which truth is often the first casualty, gives dramatic urgency to the search for "alternative" information. But, Hulbert notes, issues whose life-and-death character is less immediately visible merit the same consideration. And isn't providing alternative information a facet of a fundamental ecumenical vocation: making all churches aware of the life and witness of those whose voices are seldom heard and whose stories are seldom told?

Among many other things, the WCC's seventh assembly recommended that "churches should help to develop alternate means of communication". Specifically mentioned were "theatre, special liturgies and local, indigenous newspapers and radio". Why not add computer conferencing to this list?

To *develop* this as an alternate means of communication will not be easy. Credibility is one of the difficult issues. Another is the unjust distribution of resources, which still puts most computers and modems in the hands of people in wealthy societies. If this justice issue is not faced, the danger is strong that an alternative intended to "give a voice to the voiceless" will in fact merely give them our own voice.

July 1991

127

ON PATRIOTISM

There is abundant evidence for thinking ill of patriotism. Despots and advertisers alike offer confirmation of Samuel Johnson's well-known definition: "the last refuge of a scoundrel". And ordinary politicians often convince one that Dryden's withering comment was not far off the mark: "Never was patriot yet, but was a fool".

Having lived outside my country for almost nine years, I always feel a bit disoriented when returning to the US. That sense was much more acute during two recent visits I made there in the wake of the lavish and unashamed love for country spawned by Operation Desert Storm.

Between those two trips came the traditional end-of-the-school-year ceremonies at my youngest daughter's local Geneva primary school. Many of the children's sketches focused on the 700th anniversary of the Swiss Confederation; and the programme finished with the students singing the national hymn. In the US, many public events, including every baseball game, begin with the singing of the national anthem; by contrast, I can't remember the last time I had heard the Swiss national hymn sung in public.

Many students at our local public school are not Swiss. What, I wondered, does it mean for Elizabeth — or her Italian and French and Spanish and Portuguese classmates — to sing the Swiss national hymn? What would it mean for her to sing the national hymn of her own country (where she has spent something less than ten per cent of her life)? More to the point, what would she think it meant?

Meanwhile, the presence or absence of the feeling of love for country was having significant consequences elsewhere in Europe. Conflict erupted when Slovenia and Croatia declared independence from Yugoslavia. Voices from outside issued urgent appeals for preserving the status quo, obviously fearful of what might happen if the habit of secession were to prove contagious.

But in what can one root the sort of attachment to country — loyalty, if you will — that might hold together Yugoslavia? Can patriotism cement that which might otherwise fissure? And if such a patriotism could somehow be generated, what would prevent fools and scoundrels from taking advantage of it?

Most WCC member churches have most of their members in a single country. Within that commonality, there is wide diversity of church-state relations, and a correspondingly broad range of understandings of "patriotism".

Much of the identity of the WCC's newest member church — the China Christian Council — was forged after the missionary era in the Three-Self Patriotic Movement. Characteristic of the Armenian Apostolic Church, WCC moderator Aram Keshishian noted, "has been the close identification of the church and nation. . . . All Armenian political aspirations and questions related to human rights are echoed and manifested in the church."

Other churches display quite different attitudes towards patriotism. The Swiss churches' proposal to mark the 700th anniversary of the Confederation by a Jubilee Year seeks to turn the eyes of citizens far beyond the horizons of their own country. In the US, 1992's anniversary of 500 years since the voyage of Columbus has raised ecumenical controversy about national memory and identity.

Then there is the Single European Act, which has made Europe 1992 a symbol for a whole new understanding of the primacy of national prerogatives. Alastair Hulbert, appointed by the Church of Scotland in 1991 to serve on the staff of the Brussels-based European Ecumenical Commission on Church and Society (EECCS), notes that many European church leaders have warned that this triumph of broader horizons over narrow nationalism is itself not without risks and ambiguities.

The ecumenical movement thus provides an arena in which different notions of patriotism encounter each other. Some of this patriotism may indeed be manipulated by scoundrels; others will surely be expressed by fools.

But ecumenical encounter, it seems to me, offers two challenges here. It obliges those nervous about patriotism to think more widely and deeply about the mutual commitments and loyalties and solidarities elicited by patriotism at its best. And it asks those who are comfortable with patriotism to imagine if — and how — they could comfortably express and explain that love for their country to fellow Christians from elsewhere in the *oikoumene*.

August/September 1991

THE CONTINUATION OF HISTORY

The evidence is flimsy for what was not long ago trumpeted optimistically as "the end of history".

To be sure, the revolutionary events that shook the Soviet Union in August mean that the world will never be the same, as Ninan Koshy observes; the WCC's former international affairs director warns that it will be a long time before we can fully grasp the implications of those changes. In the Soviet Union, meanwhile, winter approaches, and old grievances, long suppressed, bubble towards the surface.

Earlier radical upheavals have left painful new problems. In some parts of Romania, at least, the fall of the Ceausescu dictatorship has if anything worsened the plight of the Roma or Gypsy people, who have become the favourite target of open hatred in the media and elsewhere.

And whether or not the relationship between Orthodox Serbians and Roman Catholic Croatians is the most difficult ecumenical situation in the world today, the confrontation in Yugoslavia, which has already taken hundreds of lives and created thousands of refugees, does not seem any more amenable to ecumenical mediation than to any other kind.

In Connecticut, the wealthiest state in the country where the "new world order" has been announced most enthusiastically, hundreds of marchers endured August heat to make the point that priorities are all out of kilter and that the massive and expensive victory of Operation Desert Storm was a diversion from the real issues that face the US.

That history goes on — and a lot of the old order survives — is not a merely political observation.

131

Steps towards drastically reducing the number of nuclear weapons the US and the Soviet Union point at each other may well ease nightmare scenarios of millions dying in an atomic holocaust. Then we are reminded that something like 40 million people will be infected with AIDS by the end of this decade.

A new realization of the need to change our lifestyle in order to preserve the environment is taking hold in many quarters. But a regional ecumenical organization warns that "the Caribbean *person* is an endangered species" — and enumerates an impressive list of obstacles to reversing that particular ecological catastrophe.

For women who are victims of often-hidden violence, any thought of a "new world order" awaits radical changes even in the place where one might have thought that a new order took hold long ago — the church.

In the face of all this grim continuity, how significant is the news that the World Council of Churches has a new programmatic structure? One is tempted to borrow Ninan Koshy's conclusion: it will be months, or maybe even years, before that question can be answered.

Unchanged by the new structure are the WCC's functions: visible unity, common witness, service of human needs, breaking down barriers between people and promoting one human family in justice and peace, renewal of the churches in unity, worship, mission and service.

The new forms taken by old realities of poverty, sickness, oppression, hatred, violence and war as history goes on suggest a continuing agenda for the churches and the ecumenical movement. The new WCC structure will be judged, finally, by how flexibly and effectively it keeps up with the reality that often the more things change, the more they remain the same.

November 1991

PRAYING FOR UNITY

In much of the world, January is when Christians of different traditions join to celebrate the Week of Prayer for Christian Unity, linking commemorations of the Confession of St Peter (the 18th) and the Conversion of St Paul (the 25th).

Resources for the Week are now prepared jointly by the WCC's Faith and Order Commission and the Pontifical Council for Promoting Christian Unity, using materials drafted by a local ecumenical group. But it was celebrated long before there was a WCC or a Vatican body to promote ecumenism. The idea originated in 1908 with Society of the Atonement founder Paul Wattson's call for an "octave for Christian unity"; its present form grows out of a 1935 appeal by French Roman Catholic Abbé Paul Couturier.

The theme and resource materials are developed internationally, but activities planned and undertaken locally are the heart of the Week of Prayer: the sheer opportunity to get acquainted with other Christians, the possibility that such contacts will encourage cooperation and commitment during the other 51 weeks of the year, the potential bubbling up and out from local parishes of a new impatience with disunity.

But to follow recent news of many churches is to be struck by the thought that intercessions offered during the Week of Prayer for Christian Unity had better be unusually fervent. In many places around the world, the prospects for Christian unity seem distinctly inauspicious.

Examples, alas, can be multiplied. Most painful, perhaps, are the divisions around the so-called uniate churches in Eastern Europe. In the US, concerted efforts are underway to overcome a serious division

133

within the National Council of Churches, but despite evident ecumenical commitment on both sides no one imagines this problem will be easy to solve.

Aggravating the overwhelming challenges the churches in South Africa must face together en route to a non-racial society are tensions within and among those churches. A Korean member of the WCC central committee suggested recently that the shadow side of the unequalled numerical growth of Christianity in his country was its unenviable distinction of leading the world in denominational splits.

Korea is far from having a monopoly on schism. And a disturbing element of recent moves by dissatisfied groups in a number of churches to form separate jurisdictions is the bitter and intemperate language, reminiscent of the anathemas of an earlier era, they use to characterize those with whom they disagree.

Also disquieting is the feeling summed up by a Christian publisher who stopped at the WCC stand at the Frankfurt Book Fair a few months ago. "Do you have any good books without the word 'ecumenical' in the title?", he wondered. The question was half-humorous, but the barb in the half that wasn't meant as a joke struck home: many people might be interested in reading about issues that concern the WCC if they didn't come wrapped in the label "ecumenical".

Is it not appropriate to suggest that some of the prayers during the Week of Prayer for Christian Unity be specific petitions for the success of what the churches are seeking to undertake in the WCC at a moment of history when such common ventures do not generate universal enthusiasm? Of course, the test of whether such prayers are sincere will be the commitments, local and global, that follow in the years to come.

January/February 1992

OBEDIENT ECUMENISM

Two things struck me as I read a recent news report of a meeting of Catholic lay people in Lausanne at which Swiss Bishop Pierre Mamie reflected on his experiences at the [Roman Catholic] Synod of Bishops of Europe.

Twice, Mamie recalled, he was gently but firmly reprimanded by the bishop sitting next to him for remarks he had made in plenary sessions: once for suggesting that the pope's use of the term "new evangelization" might be misunderstood, once for urging that one ought, when discussing abortion, to show pastoral understanding of the plight of the women affected.

The bishop was an old church leader from Eastern Europe who had spent many years in prison for his faith. Like many others, he had been totally cut off from what was happening in the church universal. Unable to experience the renewal signalled by the Second Vatican Council, his "ecclesial point of reference" was the church of his parents, before the Russian Revolution.

During those trying years, the old bishop said, his hope was sustained by his faith in Jesus Christ. And he had been comforted a great deal by "the existence of the pope, whatever his name was". Consequently, he now found it problematic to hear another bishop publicly voice an opinion which could be interpreted as diverging, no matter how modestly, from Rome.

Mamie went on to tell the meeting in Lausanne that the principal obstacle to building a new Europe is the division among Christians. Thus, for the evangelization of Europe, ecumenism "is an act of obedience to Jesus Christ".

That is a strong term for describing ecumenism. Usually, I suspect, when we use the expression "the ecumenical imperative", it is a rhetorical way of saying we think ecumenism is very important. How often do we really conceive of ecumenical involvement in the stark and uncompromising terms of obedience to Jesus Christ? Or of ecumenical non-involvement as disobedience to him? Do we not rather look on ecumenism as something we choose because it makes sense: it renders the church more effective or credible, or its absence is embarrassing?

That led to a second thought. If we do see ecumenism as a matter of obedience to Jesus Christ, what are the concrete consequences of this? And here, the story of Bishop Mamie's colleague in Rome sharpens the issue.

It seems to me beyond doubt that this bishop is a modern-day hero of faith — not of the Roman Catholic faith but of the Christian faith. Most of us hesitate even to wonder how we would have reacted under similar circumstances. But many of us would also find it strange to imagine that if we were imprisoned for our faith we might be comforted or encouraged by thinking of the bishop of Rome as a successor to St Peter.

What does it mean to obey Christ's mandate for unity alongside Christians whose faith experiences lead them to an understanding of the structure and order and role of the church so completely at odds with our own? The difficulty is more acute when that understanding has been forged and tempered in an experience of persecution. As one writer observed in *The Tablet*, "it is difficult to be even mildly critical without appearing churlish or insensitive to the suffering of martyrs."

The problem is more general. Cultural differences may strain and sometimes break the unity even among Christians who share the same confessional tradition. Personal experiences of joy and perceptions of answered prayer, as well as sorrow and trials, may lead others to expressions of Christian faith widely different from our own.

It is easy to behave ecumenically (and to congratulate ourselves for obeying the Lord's will) when ecumenism means cooperation and fellowship and solidarity with the like-minded. How do we avoid the absolutizing of our own insights and convictions that not only throws up obstacles to ecumenism but also inoculates our own faith against the possibility of growth and enrichment?

March 1992

SATURDAYS AND SUNDAYS

The denominational tradition in which I grew up could probably be described as liturgically austere. Only in the last couple of decades has awareness of the church calendar begun to penetrate through age-old suspicions that commemorating any religious festival other than Christmas, Good Friday, Easter, Ascension Day and Pentecost is dangerously close to "superstition".

As a result, the day between Good Friday and Easter Sunday has always seemed to me an awkward sort of misfit. Good Friday calls attention to the cross and Easter Sunday to the resurrection, but the Saturday between them was an enigma, a featureless pause. All four evangelists, notably John, observe that the cross and the empty tomb were separated by a sabbath day; but in dozens of Good Friday and Easter Sermons I don't recall ever hearing a preacher comment on that fact.

At the same time, the tradition in which I was reared placed heavy emphasis on the importance of observing the 52 "Lord's Days" each year. The Lord's Day was of course Sunday, the day of the resurrection — the anomalous sabbath between Good Friday and Easter having turned out to be the *last* one.

The commandment to "remember the sabbath day to keep it holy", applied to Sunday, was interpreted strictly, though already a generation ago fissures had begun to appear. Collapsing under their own weight, the rules for what should and should not be done on Sunday (playing tennis at the park was forbidden, but badminton in the back yard was tolerated) eventually died the death of a thousand qualifications.

Amused by recalling such quaint folklore from an ethnic Protes-

137

tant backwater in the US midwest in the 1950s, one is surprised to discover that the question of what is and isn't appropriate — indeed, allowed — on Sunday is an issue of some dispute in secularized Western Europe in 1992.

To be sure, current controversies have far less to do with theology than with the rights of workers, the economic power of large chain stores and the sensitive political issue of whether the European Community ought to regulate Sunday trading too.

Anomalies abound. It is legal in London to buy a pizza on Sunday — and a sports tabloid to read while you're eating it. But it's against the law to buy fish-and-chips or a Bible. Meanwhile, back in liberated Western Michigan, parking lots at shopping malls are packed on Sunday afternoons.

Orthodox theologian and ecumenist Nicholas Lossky describes an understanding of the Saturday between Good Friday and Easter as the "sabbath *par excellence*". To take that seriously is to turn on its head the casuistry about what is or is not permitted on "the Lord's Day". If the sabbath rest of Christ in the tomb was dynamic, as Lossky says, if it consisted in *working for salvation,* then our following him implies that "the day of rest is a privileged moment for practising an active remembrance of the Lord".

The heart of understanding what the Lord's Day is about, then, consists in asking not what we should *not* do, but what we should do: "practising justice and mercy, living out our love for the neighbour" — the very sort of thing that earned Jesus the reputation of being a sabbath-desecrator during his earthly life.

And then, as Lossky suggests, another question follows inevitably: on which day of our lives are we *not* called to live in the light of this sabbath?

The "liberal" or "liberated" retort to the strict and legalistic codes for Sunday observance in my youth was that, "after all, *every* day is the Lord's day". Seen in the light of the sabbath day that builds a bridge from Good Friday to Easter, that argument would seem to set forth a higher, not a lower standard of conduct.

April 1992

138

WHERE TO DRAW THE LINE

Next month my denomination faces a severe test of unity. Its annual synod will decide whether or not to ratify an earlier decision by changing the church order to allow women to hold any office in the church.

The issue has been before the assemblies of the church for nearly twenty years. Discussion has centred on how to interpret biblical passages that might be seen as bearing on whether or not women may hold office in the church.

From both sides have come voices of pain and often anger. People have said they will leave the church in which they were baptized if the decision goes one way or the other; some have already left.

Whatever the synod decides, some will conclude that the church has gone astray — either those who believe the Bible forbids ordaining women or those who believe that the tradition of ordaining only men absolutizes first-century cultural realities that are indefensible in the twentieth.

No matter what the decision, some will see a church (in the terms of Samuel Stone's familiar hymn) "by schism rent asunder", others a church "by heresies distressed". And many watching from outside will display "a scornful wonder".

The plight of this denomination is a parable of what makes the quest for church unity so difficult.

It is tempting to quote to both sides the words Oliver Cromwell addressed to the Church of Scotland more than three centuries ago: "I beseech you, in the bowels of Christ, think it possible you may be mistaken."

Should infants be baptized? Should the eucharist be celebrated once a week, or once a month, or four times a year? Is violence ever justified in the effort to reverse injustice?

Let us discuss all these issues. Let us take them seriously. Let us even argue passionately about them. But let all who take part in those discussions do so thinking it possible that they may be mistaken.

I can imagine maintaining Christian fellowship with those who hold a different view from mine on baptism or the frequency of eucharist or the just war theory. Why, then, when thinking of how Cromwell's plea applies to the present case, is it only to those on one side of the issue that I want to pose the challenge? Not because their view is at variance with convictions I have always held. Not, I trust, because I imagine I am never mistaken.

Probably it is because I believe that if the other view were to prevail, it would not only work against the renewal of the church but continue to legitimate injustice within the church. To qualify this conviction by the rider that I "may be mistaken" seems to weaken it too much — at the expense of justice for others.

Perhaps, however, the more important issue for the unity of the church is not "might I be mistaken about this or that conviction?", but rather, "might I be mistaken in considering this issue as one over which differences of opinion make it appropriate *at this moment* to break the unity of the church?"

Not that this is an easier question to answer. Nor does it tell delegates to the synod of my church how to vote. But it does demand an acknowledgment that the unity and renewal of the church requires continuous openness to change from everybody, that change takes more time than we usually imagine and that renewal comes finally as a gift of the Spirit, not just as a result of the success of the "right side" in changing the mind of those who are "mistaken".

May 1992

THE BURDEN OF PAPER

On a recent flight to the US, wedged into a seat that might have comfortably accommodated the average jockey or ten-year-old, and further immobilized by a tray table with the uncollected remains of dinner, I chanced to read the small print on the customs declaration.

This is the form on which incoming travellers tell customs officials what they are bringing into the country, itemizing anything which might be subject to duty. It warns of grave consequences for untruthful visitors.

But the small print had nothing to do with sealing the country's borders against smugglers. Rather, it was a "statement required by CFR 1320.21", to wit: "The estimated average burden associated with this collection of information is three minutes per respondent or recordkeeper depending on individual circumstances.

"Comments concerning the accuracy of this burden estimate and suggestions for reducing this burden should be directed to the US Customs Service, Paperwork Management Branch, Washington DC 20229, and to the Office of Management and Budget, Paperwork Reduction Project (1515-0041), Washington DC 20503."

After a second reading, I figured out what this meant: "We think it will take you about three minutes to fill out this form. If you think it takes longer than that — or that it shouldn't take as long as it does, please let us know. (But you still have to fill out the form.)"

Reading such matchlessly bureaucratic prose while your legs are going to sleep stimulates a range of dyspeptic questions. Exactly who "estimated" this "average burden"? For that matter, what is an "estimated average"? Isn't it precisely the point of an "average" to take account of "individual circumstances"? What do they mean by "individual circumstances" anyway: a ballpoint pen that doesn't work or excessive scrupulousness about breaking regulations you don't understand?

Why don't they tell you that you'll have time to fill out the form twenty times over while waiting in line for a customs agent? And wouldn't it reduce the government's paperwork burden if it had only one rather than two offices looking into this matter?

I thought about this recently when the commissions for each of the WCC's four new programme units met in Evian, France, to discuss the focus of the Council's activities over the next half dozen years. In the back of my mind was the stack of periodicals and papers and letters and memos accumulating on my desk in Geneva. And if anything was certain about the meeting in Evian, it was that I would carry back even more piles of paper.

Wouldn't it be nice if the World Council of Churches had a "Paperwork Reduction Project"?

That the ecumenical movement produces too much paper is a proposition that would probably elicit unanimous agreement across confessions and cultures, from men and women of all ages and nationalities. Everyone would say "Amen" to the observation that the language of no ecumenical document on social ethics has ever achieved the succinct and compelling power of "you shall love your neighbour as yourself". No one would dispute that most ecumenical gatherings could well preface their verbose conclusions with a quotation from Abraham Lincoln at Gettysburg: "The world will little note nor long remember what we say here."

Yet paperwork reduction at ecumenical meetings would face difficulties inherent in ecumenism itself. Sometimes ecumenical documents are long and unwieldy because of the broad spectrum of experiences, concerns and convictions they are obliged to encompass. As more and more voices are heard and taken seriously, the agenda is complicated, agreed statements more difficult to achieve and setting priorities — which always involves saying no to some — more painful.

Ecumenical discernment means distinguishing what is confusing from what is merely confused. The estimated average burden of doing that is greater than one would wish, but the alternative may not be the brevity that is the soul of wit, but the brevity of the sound-bite.

June 1992

THE OLD WAYS

One of the endless variations of a familiar old joke is what might be called the "confessional" version: How many *(fill in the name of the denomination of your choice)* does it take to change a light bulb? The answer is four: one to turn in the new bulb and three to say they really liked the old one better.

In fact, I first heard this version applied to Lutherans, but if you seriously imagine that disgruntlement over change in the church is specific to the heirs of Martin Luther, I suggest you read the accounts of what happens in just about any denomination when it decides to introduce new liturgical forms or a new hymnbook.

There are many reasons that most of us "like the old ways better" — not least the way nostalgia fosters glorification of the past by blurring the edges of our memories. Besides, we get used to the old ways of doing things. In a complex world that throws up more than enough challenges to our coping, trying out a new way of thinking or acting may seem like too much of an effort, if not an outright risk.

I'm writing these lines in the midst of the hassle at the Earth Summit in Rio over the intransigence and isolation of the United States about endorsing the international environmental agreements being considered there. Quite apart from the question of whether the US government is merely being open about achieving an outcome that certain other powerful and wealthy countries are aiming at with more subtlety, its position does seem to reflect a peculiar attachment to "the old way of doing things".

Trying to do things a new way is a familiar theme. Sometimes this is a deliberate response to changing circumstances. Orthodox Christians in post-revolutionary Romania are faced by the bewildering possibilities and risks of entirely new ways of participating in the renewal of society. In a Methodist church in downtown Johannesburg, dramatic changes in South African society and in the composition of the congregation itself are presenting the new senior minister with a panoply of opportunities and hazards.

Other new ways of doing things are forged out of crises of conscience or conviction. For some Christians, the way international trade continues to widen the gap between poor and rich has motivated a determined search for a new way of conducting trade between countries. An ecumenical veteran who found himself in a surprising position of political leadership at the age of 75 responded to a crisis within his jurisdiction by standing on the constitution. He lost his job because his superiors liked the old way — ignoring the constitution — better.

Sometimes the appearance of a new way of doing things — a "New World Order" — may camouflage reaffirmation of existing power structures by those who enjoy the advantages the old way of doing things brought them.

The jury is still out on all these attempts to find new ways of doing things. A resurgence of hope and faith within the Romanian Orthodox Church does not in one stroke wipe away the forty-year legacy of economic ruin and social disintegration visited upon that unhappy country. The amount of money transferred from North to South through "alternative trade" sounds substantial until you compare the figure with the volume of conventional trade; and, as our article makes clear, alternative trade itself is not problem-free.

The ecumenical movement builds on the visionary heritage of pioneers who saw that the old way of doing things — endlessly fracturing the body of Christ — contradicts the gospel we proclaim. Much about the contemporary world, however, suggests that new life is being breathed into this model of fragmentation. The lines of division may be different, but the pain and the consequences of separation are no less acute.

Perhaps the greatest challenge for the movement in the years ahead is to discover how the old ways of healing divisions can be renewed and supplemented by new ways of doing things ecumenically.

July 1992

LET THE CHURCH BE THE CHURCH

Four ecumenical organizations — the WCC and the US, Korean and South African national councils of churches — recently joined in an intensive three-day visit to Los Angeles at the end of June.

WCC staff member Barney Pityana called it "a witness of the churches around the world to the churches and people of Los Angeles". He said violence and property destruction that broke out when four white Los Angeles policemen were acquitted of brutality in the Rodney King case highlight an issue touching the entire country — long neglect of the cities and the effects this has on the poor people who live there.

The visit included several unique moments:

- Small teams of visitors attended a dozen "listening posts" throughout the metropolitan area, including one in the predominantly white suburb of Simi Valley, where the trial of the four policemen took place.
- A "very honest encounter" between Korean and African Americans in the presence of NCCK and SACC representatives "raised possibilities for both communities to look together at the source of the alienation they both feel", Pityana said. Korean American businesses in South-Central Los Angeles suffered heavy losses during the uprising.
- Several visiting church leaders spent three hours with leaders of two street gangs, the Crips and the Bloods. NCC general secretary Joan Campbell highlighted two elements from that unusual conversation.

One was the gang leaders' insistence that instead of welfare the government should support economic development: job opportunities in the neighbourhood, local ownership of stores and industries, nursery schools, day-care centres.

When she asked what they wanted from the church, they told her they were looking for "spiritual leadership and help in finding God". They also made it clear that they want the church to "live up to the gospel".

"Let the church be the church" is a theme associated with the ecumenical Conference on Church, Community and State (Oxford, 1937). It is startling and instructive now to hear it echoed by members of urban street gangs.

Like any catchy slogan, of course, it is prone to misinterpretation. In 1937, Niels Ehrenström wrote in *A History of the Ecumenical Movement,* some saw in these words "the triumph of ecclesiastical introversion", the capitulation of "the prophetic and missionary spirit" to "sacerdotalism and ecclesiasticism". For many people in 1992, "let the church be the church" no doubt sounds like "keep the church out of politics", "don't let it rock the boat or disturb the status quo".

Oxford itself was clear what it means for the church to be the church: not only "to witness for God, to preach his word, to confess the faith before men and women, to teach both young and old to observe the divine commandments", but also "to serve the nation and the state by proclaiming the will of God as the supreme standard to which all human wills must be subject and all human conduct must conform".

Convincing residents of South-Central Los Angeles that the church is ready to be the church in that costly sense will not be easy. Their scepticism about political leaders also applies to religious leaders. A black Muslim told the team: "They don't fulfill their promises or live up to expectations. We need preachers and imams and community leaders who are accountable to the people."

Can the churches in the US proclaim "the will of God as the supreme standard" to those within and outside their membership who want to turn their back on the realities of what decaying urban centres are doing to people created in God's image? Are churches around the world ready to offer them ecumenical encouragement and support —

and in turn to be encouraged and supported in their own efforts to be the church?

August/September 1992

FIVE HUNDRED YEARS

To be honest, I suppose I haven't thought very deeply this year about the voyage of Christopher Columbus.

Paradoxically, this may be the result of over-exposure to "the 500th". Within the WCC and elsewhere, there have been so many reminders of "1492" that it is easy to assume one has already come to terms with it. The pervasive symbolism of the anniversary becomes an excuse to avoid substantive questions about the event and its half-millennium of consequences.

Perhaps it also has to do with the fact that Columbus never really captivated my attention. A few memorized couplets *("Behind him lay the grey Azores,/Behind the Gates of Hercules,/Before him not the ghost of shores,/Before him only shoreless seas . . .")* of Joaquin Miller still rattle around in my head after 35 years. The point of this edifying verse was hammered home in the refrain, *"Sail on! Sail on!"* But for one growing up far from the ocean, naval metaphors for the importance of persisting against all odds were not as engaging as stories of doughty nineteenth-century Dutch-American pioneers carving out a *kolonie* in western Michigan's inhospitable climate and terrain.

One was vaguely aware that the name "Columbus" lived on in obscure patriotic anthems, the nation's capital, a western river and a university in New York. But one never imagined, for example, that the 15th-century explorer was the spiritual ancestor of Columbia University in the same way as the spirit of a 16th-century reformer lived on in Calvin College.

Even later, when I came to recognize the plight of the descendants of those who were there to meet Columbus, I'm not certain I linked the shameful history of westward expansion in my own country with the whole Eurocentric project of "discovery" and conquest and "sailing on" epitomized by Columbus. These painful accounts of cheating and slaughtering Indigenous people spoke of particular acts of greed and evil — to be repented of and even compensated for — but not of something woven into the fabric of my own cultural heritage.

Reading two articles recently has belatedly drawn my attention to some of the deeper implications of the events of the past 500 years. One is an essay by Elsa Tamez, in the October *Ecumenical Review,* "The Indigenous Peoples Are Evangelizing Us". Tamez, who teaches at the Latin American Biblical Seminary in Costa Rica, says it is high time "to pause and listen; to reflect maturely and with open minds on the actual realities on which Christianity has set its seal; to assume the consequences of an invasion legitimated by a 'Christian' theology".

What she asks us to reflect on is the more painful because of how bluntly it appears in the historical record. Columbus speaks in one breath of "converting a multitude of peoples to our Holy Faith and winning great domains and riches and all their peoples for Spain"; Cortés writes that "as we were carrying the banner of the cross, God granted us such victory that we killed many people without receiving harm ourselves"; Garcia de Toledo offers a no-nonsense version of double predestination — where there were mines and treasures "the gospel was brought swiftly and competently", where Indigenous people were poor no "soldier or captain nor even a minister of the gospel" bothered to go; Chief Tecpanécatl builds a temple to "the new God the Spaniards have brought to us" and urges his people to be baptized "and perhaps then they will not kill us".

Another article, by WCC inter-religious relations staff member Hans Ucko, makes clear how much the consequences of the evangelization Tamez describes remain on the agenda. Just as the Christian churches in this century have had to adjust to renewal in other world religions, so now there are signs of renewal of the Indigenous religious faith and vision suppressed by the coming of the Europeans 500 years ago.

Such a renewal complicates already ecumenically difficult questions of interfaith dialogue and "gospel and culture". Coming to terms with this in the years ahead will demand even more reserves of the grace to "pause and listen".

November 1992

THE MINISTRY OF RECONCILIATION

A familiar biblical explanation of the significance of the event Christians celebrate at this season is that of 2 Corinthians 5:18. Through him who came at Bethlehem, "God reconciled us to himself"; and God "has given us the ministry of reconciliation".

Changes in South Africa have focused the churches' attention on reconciliation. The interview with WCC general secretary Emilio Castro and the account of an ecumenical visit there in September set in bold relief the pitfalls of easy reconciliation and the unbreakable link between reconciliation and persistent solidarity with the victims of apartheid's unspeakable suffering.

"Reconciliation" between oppressor and oppressed comes to nothing if it merely creates an illusory calm during which oppressors can find more socially acceptable ways to serve themselves. Years of solidarity with suffering people in South Africa have given credibility to the churches' present witness to and engagement for reconciliation. Forgetting or suspending that solidarity now would empty of meaning any call for nonviolence and negotiated solutions.

The long-awaited peace agreement in Mozambique raises questions of reconciliation in a country ruined by a dozen years of brutal civil war. The ministry facing churches there, under the leadership of the Christian Council of Mozambique (CCM), is breathtaking.

It is inspiring and humbling to read of the CCM general secretary's vision of former enemies working side by side at the village level to rebuild homes and schools. The magnitude of the miracle of reconciliation for which Mozambican Christians are working and praying is evident in the question cited elsewhere in the article:

"What does reconciliation mean for a woman who has seen her enemies kill her husband or mother and burn her home?"

Reconciliation inevitably came up when Christians in the countries around the Baltic Sea met in Lund to discuss issues of race and ethnicity long kept beneath the surface. Simply put, the problem is "how to deal with the past without committing fresh injustices".

The situation of all these churches highlights three elements of the ministry of reconciliation. In the first place, it is not something the churches can take up or ignore as they see fit. For, as WCC Programme to Combat Racism director Barney Pityana says, churches are "made up of the same people who in their daily lives are having to contend with the conflicts in society" — in addition to which they are always being solicited by political forces looking to co-opt them.

Second, it is a ministry that requires hard work. That is why the Lund consultation spent time talking about strategies for change. That is why the Christian Council of Mozambique set in motion a detailed Peace and Reconciliation Programme long before a peace accord was signed. That is why South African churches welcome ecumenical "monitors" from abroad during the period of transition in their country.

Third, it is a ministry that requires a conviction that God's grace can bring about a miracle, that lives can be changed, that forgiveness is possible even when it is difficult, that (in the apostle's words) "those who live might live no longer for themselves, but for him who died and was raised for them" (2 Corinthians 5:15).

Those who accept the ministry of reconciliation understand the challenge of the Christmas season. As Emilio Castro's Christmas message puts it, "Our celebration of Christmas in the midst of a cruel world must not be an act of selfishness that cuts us off from this world but a sign of hope, a call to love, an act of solidarity."

December 1992

151

PEOPLE DIE

In John's vision of the New Jerusalem, trees beside the river bear leaves "for the healing of the nations" (Revelation 22:12).

To look around the world today (including Jerusalem) is to be reminded of more terrifying imagery from the last book of the Bible — visions of conflict and oppression, of famine and pestilence, of a "pale green horse" whose rider's name is Death (Revelation 6:8).

Nowhere has the need for the healing of nations seemed clearer this past year than in the former Yugoslavia. It may well be that public awareness of this conflict has been heightened because it is in Europe, while other horrifying situations multiply the agony of even more people in places the international media and their paying consumers are wont to ignore. Yet all this attention has not put an end to the suffering.

Central to the "healing of the nations" in the former Yugoslavia is the "healing of memories". But the course of events so far, says a joint statement on Bosnia-Herzegovina by the officers of the WCC and the executive committee of the Conference of European Churches, is in exactly the opposite direction:

"Ultra-nationalist policies claim to address fears which are projected from historical memories onto an uncertain future. At the same time, they accelerate a process of bringing about what is feared: massive killing, mass rape of women, widespread suffering and torture and large-scale displacement of the population. Passions are manipulated to excuse or even justify atrocities. But instead of exorcising fear, this perpetuates its destructive grip." Among lost memories is the history of periods of "constructive living together" in the Balkans.

The WCC-CEC statement reiterates some basic ecumenical convictions in the face of the alarming repercussions of the conflict on inter-communal relations elsewhere in the world: "We are committed not to allow the conflict to suggest in any way a confrontation between 'Christendom' and the 'Islamic' ummah (community). This war is not on behalf of 'Christian Europe' against Islam."

The ecumenical leaders go on to insist that "enforcing separation or accentuating antagonisms" cannot solve the problems of a pluralist society in crisis or transition. They underline earlier calls for an immediate halt to hostilities and negotiations without preconditions, commitments "to be peacemakers and agents of reconciliation" and appeals to the international community to redouble efforts — despite the complexity of the situation — to bring the fighting to an end and to provide immediate refuge for its victims until then.

And, they say, "we cannot surrender to a cynical political realism which considers what has happened thus far as irreversible".

During a WCC consultation in Geneva, a Bosnian Muslim passed along a copy of a poem by 1987 Nobel literature laureate Joseph Brodsky. It begins:

"As you pour yourself a scotch, crush a roach, or check your watch, as your hand adjusts your tie, people die.

"In the towns with funny names, hit by bullets, caught in flames, by and large not knowing why, people die. . . ."

Brodsky's last line jolts anyone tempted by "cynical political realism" or apathy to stop hoping for the healing of nations, to stop even thinking about this awful war:

"Time, whose sharp bloodthirsty quill parts the killer from those who kill, will pronounce the latter tribe as your type."

The title of the poem is "A Tune for Bosnia". In fact, it is a tune for everywhere.

January/February 1993

THE "UNFASHIONABLE POOR"

In November 1974 the first issue of *One World* included an article about gross human rights violations in Equatorial Guinea. There were follow-up pieces in several succeeding issues; then, for another twenty years, Equatorial Guinea — a country many readers would probably have trouble finding on a map — did not reappear in our pages. The painful truth is that in the past two decades the situation of its people has not improved decisively.

There are other countries seldom in the forefront of international media coverage or ecumenical attention: Mauritania, where Christians are helping a Muslim country cope with environmental refugees; Namibia, celebrating the third anniversary of independence this month; Congo, where, despite its own difficulties, thousands of people fled renewed fighting in neighbouring Zaïre in February; and Togo.

Critics sometimes fault international ecumenical declarations and denunciations for singling out some situations while appearing silent and inactive about others. During the cold war, the WCC was often accused of operating with a double standard: a penchant, alleged to be ideologically rooted, for focusing on the misdeeds of "the West" and its "clients" while ignoring equal if not worse atrocities elsewhere.

The end of the cold war has not ended debates about the merits of the WCC policy of avoiding public declarations about countries where church leaders fear this would damage the interests of their churches, for it has never been only the now-fallen regimes in Europe which raised this issue.

A more nuanced version of the "selectivity" critique charges that, while poverty-stricken and suffering people in certain countries attract a lot of ecumenical concern, there are also the "unfashionable

154

poor", dying of tyranny, hunger and disease far from the attention of both the media and the international Christian community.

Ironically, Somalia has often been cited as an example of the "unfashionable poor". That this unhappy country has seldom been off the front pages in the past several months doesn't disprove the point but sets it in bold relief, underlining suspicions already voiced that when the outside forces have wearied of their mission of mercy Somalia's suffering will again be relegated to international obscurity.

The bitter reality that those who are suffering must in effect compete for attention from those who might help to alleviate their misery has been underlined dramatically by the war in the former Yugoslavia and growing awareness of the vast needs throughout Eastern and Central Europe.

It would be perverse to suggest that since we cannot help everyone we may as well decide to help no one, though many people often seem to act according to that principle. Yet our inevitable selectivity is a useful warning against self-congratulation, the temptation to assess too generously the merits of our engagements on behalf of persons elsewhere.

Publishing or reading some short items about how Christians and churches are responding to these little-known situations scarcely qualifies as a gesture of solidarity. And the number of situations *One World* does *not* cover far exceeds the few that it does. Yet maybe these stories can help not only to inform our intercessions for some courageous fellow-Christians but also to stimulate hard thinking about what solidarity means in a "new world order" which daily makes evident how much the need for solidarity exceeds our ability to feel or express it.

March 1993

NO INSTANT CONVERSIONS

A professor with whom I once took a course in Old Testament did not allow his biblical literalism to exclude an occasional allegorical interpretation.

One example was 1 Samuel 13:19-22: "Now there was no smith to be found throughout all the land of Israel; for the Philistines said, 'The Hebrews must not make swords or spears for themselves'; so all the Israelites went down to the Philistines to sharpen their ploughshares, mattocks, axes or sickles." As a result, when a skirmish broke out, "neither sword nor spear was to be found in the possession of any of the people".

Not only was this an historical note about Israel's slowness to join the Iron Age, the professor opined, it also foreshadowed the plight of 20th-century conservative Protestantism. For in the absence of solidly evangelical graduate schools, students were doing advanced study in "liberal-radical" faculties — sharpening their tools and weapons of spiritual warfare among "modernists", the contemporary equivalent of the Philistines.

Today, military metaphors, embedded in the language of Christian faith from St Paul to "Onward, Christian Soldiers", are largely out of favour, though the issue of the church's role in countering the global arms race is very much alive.

Ironically, at its heart lies a central reality of the Christian faith: conversion. "Conversion" is the economists' technical term for beating swords into ploughshares and spears into pruning hooks, or, more precisely, turning sword and spear factories into firms producing goods for peace and prosperity.

Daunting as the problems of retooling, retraining and refinancing may be, the obstacles facing conversion in this sense are not just technical and economic. What is also at stake are habits of the mind and heart which allow most of us to gloss over or ignore the realities of using weapons of war.

One reality is the waste they involve. That was set in sharp relief for me long ago when I watched something called a "night-fire demonstration" in the army. Several companies of recruits were marched into the countryside. Once darkness fell, the range came alive with small arms fire, automatic weapons, grenade launchers, mortars and rockets, anti-tank weapons. Tracer bullets flashed across the sky and the ground shook with explosion after explosion.

The exercise did not pretend to any tactical, ideological or even training purpose: it was simply a prodigiously expensive fireworks display staged for a couple of hundred young men in the middle of Missouri. Not once was the word "kill" even mentioned.

More serious than our acceptance of waste is our tolerance of the sheer quantity of killing that happens when these weapons are put to tactical use. While writing these lines I paused to listen to the news on the BBC. The first two items on this Sunday morning in March included virtually identical phrases — *"in which thousands of people are said to have lost their lives"*. These were not stories about Somalia or the former Yugoslavia, where daily news stories offer a kind of running tally of death. They were about Afghanistan and Angola, where wars were supposed to have ended months ago.

The conversion that came to Saul on the Damascus Road was exceptional. Churches working for the changes of heart and mind that are indispensable for ending the arms race should probably expect no blinding flashes of light.

April 1993

157

LIMITING DIVERSITY

It's a useful exercise for a *One World* editor to page through recent issues and classify the contents by geography, church tradition and ecumenical programmes and concerns. Such a survey can indicate how adequately the magazine is reflecting the diversity of an ecumenical reality that ranges from major global events examining theological differences to projects in using video to help marginalized people to help themselves, from agonizing with a church trying to minister in wartime to expressing solidarity with victims of peacetime violence.

Such diverse subject matter makes it interesting to edit *One World*, even if ten yearly issues of a 24-page magazine can never do justice to the variety of Christian experience and testimony in the *oikoumene*.

When we speak of diversity in the ecumenical movement it is usually positively. We cherish the ideal of inclusive community in which fellowship is shared without regard to all sorts of characteristics and conditions that divide the human community. To picture that fellowship, we use images like the mosaic, whose total splendour depends on the differences among the individual components.

Perhaps the most vivid experience of diversity in the WCC context comes in worship. Often those attending WCC meetings find the sensitive integration into worship of elements from many traditions and styles and languages and countries the most memorable thing about being there.

Maybe we are lured by the experience of ecumenical worship into an abstract and romantic view of diversity which brushes off the question why the "good and pleasant" expression of "kindred together in unity" (to paraphrase Psalm 133) in ecumenical worship often seems to have trouble surviving the move from sanctuary to meeting hall.

A preparatory document for the assembly of the Conference of European Churches included the intriguing suggestion that the recent rapid upheavals in the world require us to develop not only a "theology of change" but also a "theology of disagreement", in order "to facilitate ways of living together in our diversity".

The question of how an ecumenical body, which exists because of the differences and disagreements among its members, can live with those differences and disagreements was raised in sharp form at the WCC's 1991 Canberra assembly, eliciting repeated references to the notion of "limits to diversity".

The affirmation that there are limits to the diversity encompassed by the WCC is warranted by the WCC's constitution. It begins with a Basis, to which churches wishing to become members must agree. It sets forth the functions for which the Council was formed and the procedures by which it conducts its business, thus outlining an agenda that not everyone may accept.

It seems to me that the problem with accenting the notion of "limits to diversity" is an almost irresistible tendency to specify these limits with actual people and groups whom we would like to keep out in mind. Our appreciation of diversity may be abstract, but our ventures in setting limits to it tend to be all too concrete.

The solution, according to a recent WCC consultation, is not to say that "anything goes". In ethics and theology, there are "sincere and serious differences" among Christians and there are "boundaries" where "the being of the church is at stake". But precisely because the stakes are so high, coming to terms with diversity is a question of serious struggle, not snap judgments.

May 1993

A CERTAIN POISONED SWEETNESS

For people who grew up with the cold war, the paradigm of confrontation is perhaps the 1962 Cuban missile crisis. The very metaphor used by the US secretary of state to announce that the crisis had been defused — "we were standing eyeball-to-eyeball and the other fellow just blinked" — evoked the roots of the word "confrontation" in the Latin *frons,* forehead.

Newly available documents about that superpower confrontation suggest that there were good reasons for apocalyptic fears during those tense October days three decades ago. Maybe that helps to explain the hesitancy many people today feel about confrontation. Even apart from the threat of nuclear holocaust, there are all too many cases in our world in which neither side blinks and events go spinning out of control into catastrophe.

Some would suggest that the ecumenical movement is infected by, if not built on, a misguided distaste for confrontation. Critics of conciliar ecumenism have argued that the affirmations of the Basis of the WCC and many other ecumenical organizations are too few, casting the net too widely, and that this is then compounded by a refusal to confront member churches who seem to be straying from even those minimal standards. Others would say that the agonizing slowness of achieving convergence on church-dividing theological issues is a consequence of this avoidance of confrontation. Reluctant to have anyone disagree with what we have to say, we end up saying very little.

Not that the ecumenical movement shies away from all confrontation. Several articles in this issue describe exactly the opposite reality. In acknowledging the tangled links of racism and economics, churches and ecumenical groups often courageously confront vested interests.

160

World Vision minces no words in its confrontation of the evil of land-mines — or in its insistence that taking such advocacy positions is built into its understanding of Christian mission.

To be sure, confrontation may not immediately bring the hoped-for results, as is sadly evident from the experience of many communicators in Africa that those who govern Africa do not take kindly to criticism. Painful as it may be, genuine confrontation (unlike the catharsis of firing indignant salvos at easy targets) is a prerequisite for forgiveness, suggests German theologian Geiko Müller-Fahrenholz.

But confronting common foes — violence, injustice, oppression, the burden of the past — is not the same as confronting others within the ecumenical fellowship.

There are good reasons to be wary of confrontation within the Christian family. Too much confrontation grows out of a confusion between one's own understanding of the truth and the truth itself. Unlike St Paul, who opposed Peter "to his face", many Christian confrontationalists prefer a different stance — behind the back. Too often confrontation has more to do with a combative personality than an unswerving commitment to the truth.

To those who enjoy confrontation, John Calvin, no stranger to theological polemics, offers a clear warning. Commenting on the difficulties of obeying the commandment not to bear false witness against a neighbour, he observes how "we delight in a certain poisoned sweetness experienced in ferreting out and in disclosing the evils of others".

The taste of that "certain poisoned sweetness" sells newspapers and magazines. But the kind of confrontation it reflects erodes Christian community rather than building it up.

June 1993

161

PROPHETIC COURAGE

"Could you explain Cambodia, Israel and Yugoslavia to us?" The breathtaking request came from my daughter, who was studying with some friends for a final examination in geography the next day.

The test would focus on four topics covered in class. For reasons unknown I was mercifully exempted from questions about the fourth — the international debt crisis. The other three were daunting enough.

I could hardly say no. When I protested that by no stretch of the imagination was I an expert on any of the three countries, Amy reminded me that I had visited Belgrade only a couple of weeks earlier. Though tempted to retort that nothing could have convinced me more of my lack of qualifications to speak about the former Yugoslavia, I did my best to answer their questions, most of which had to do with names, dates, the sequence of events and developments during the two days since their last class meeting.

Any amount of writing cannot "*explain* Yugoslavia". Indeed, the more one learns about this situation the more sceptically one looks at any proffered "explanation" of it.

In the face of such complexity, is it possible for the churches — within or outside the situation — to say a clear and courageous prophetic word?

For those of us who do not share the tangle of historical memories at the root of this conflict, the three easiest ways to deal with our own perplexity are perhaps partisanship, cynicism or resignation.

The partisan decides in favour of the cause of one side in the conflict and dismisses as false propaganda any arguments against that choice. The cynic, avowing that there is more than enough evil on every side, calls down "a plague on all their houses". The strategy of res-ignation concludes that the situation cannot be resolved and that the only hope is that the warring parties will eventually give up the fight from sheer exhaustion.

None of these approaches to resolving our perplexity seems to re-flect the commitment to justice without which, the churches have said time and again, peace cannot come. Yet after seeing pictures of the brutality and horror of this war mirrored in the faces of suffering peo-ple, how can we say no more than that the situation is too compli-cated and ambiguous to make any judgments? Is that not an almost obscene intellectual self-indulgence?

Could it be that the clear prophetic word the churches are called to speak at this moment is a modest one — a persistent reminder that violence can only aggravate the problem, an unyielding insistence that if negotiations have not yet produced a solution they must not be abandoned but continue, a tireless appeal on behalf of the human rights and human dignity of all, especially innocent civilians? The very modesty of such an appeal perhaps demands courage of a different sort from the vigorous denunciation of powerful oppressors to which we are accustomed.

Along with this ecumenical prophetic task comes a pastoral and priestly one. It includes ministry to those who are suffering, no matter how limited our resources, and equipping churches and other reli-gious communities in the area for their own ministry of reconciliation and mercy.

And if we have the courage, it includes daring to keep on praying for peace with justice even if we have no idea what that might look like.

July 1993

TRYING SOMETHING DIFFERENT

The "mega-church" phenomenon began to flourish in the US in the 1970s.

This was the heyday of the controversial "church growth" approach to mission, with its insistence that in judging its evangelism efforts a church should not ignore the factor of how many people decide to affiliate with it.

In a sense, the mega-church represents a triumph of church growth theory at the parish level, though the old geographical connotations of the word "parish" don't play much of a role. Some mega-churches indeed centre on their "television ministry". Most surround their contemporary suburban buildings (or "physical plants") with vast parking lots to attract commuting worshippers.

A friend once observed how the televisual splendour of the mega-churches must arouse envy in struggling pastors of less well-to-do congregations: "They have fountains in their sanctuary; all we have is water in the basement."

Some of these large congregations in fact organize seminars and training institutes where pastors are invited to learn how to replicate such expansion and expansiveness in their own setting.

European congregations reflect a variety of models of mission (most quite different from the "mega-church"). They put varying degrees of emphasis on the typical categories for talking about how congregations reach out in mission — through liturgy, fellowship, service, spirituality. The common element in them is that dissatisfaction with the way things were produced a readiness to try something different.

These snapshots of local mission efforts are not presented as "export models", as though curious pastors might stream to Penrhys or

Akademgorodok or Valdosende to "see how it's done". Yet they recall questions familiar to anyone who has ever given much thought to the present and future of his or her own congregation:

- From where do the creative ideas leading to real change at the congregational level come? How often do they result from a deliberate search, involving long-range planning committees who draft and redraft "vision" and "mission" statements?
- The concept of "success" is often contrasted with "faithfulness". But even congregations that are inoculated against gross and worldly notions of "success" must ask themselves, "Have we succeeded in being faithful?" That means some kind of self-evaluation. In doing that, how does a congregation balance caution and rigour on the one hand and openness and readiness to make mistakes on the other?
- To some extent, what is new in a changing congregation grows out of the old and is rooted in it. But how does a changing congregation continue to minister to those members — "the faithful" — who have become accustomed to the old and like it better?
- In what ways can and should a changing congregation support and be supported by (but also criticize and be criticized by) the forms which the church takes outside of the local parish — locally, nationally and globally?

In whatever conventional or contemporary shape, the immediate experience of Christian community at the local level is fundamental.

August/September 1993

PILGRIMS' PROGRESS

Not surprisingly, the metaphor of pilgrimage was often used during the WCC's Fifth World Conference on Faith and Order in Santiago de Compostela, Spain. For hundreds of years this city has been one of Europe's best-known destinations for pilgrims.

To be sure, many who took part in the Faith and Order conference do not share the religious ethos associated with journeying to a site whose sacredness is linked to the relics of an apostle or saint (even if they would hesitate to dismiss such pilgrimages in the unfriendly terms of the Augsburg Confession: "childish and useless works").

But the image is intriguing. One might suggest three ways in which the idea of the ecumenical movement as pilgrimage can shed light on what happened in Santiago and, more importantly, on what needs to happen wherever Christians continue to tolerate broken fellowship and indeed introduce new disharmonies.

The first point is etymological. The dictionary traces the English word "pilgrim" to a Latin root meaning "being abroad". Anyone may be called a pilgrim, said Rossetti, "who leaveth the place of his birth". There is something inherently *foreign* about a pilgrimage.

If newcomers to the ecumenical pilgrimage do not recognize its "foreignness" and thus fail to take with utter seriousness the diversity of Christian languages, thought-forms and experiences they will encounter, it will be *alienating* in the true sense of the word. But it is perhaps also a besetting temptation of the ecumenically experienced to forget that this pilgrimage is taking them into foreign territory where they do not make the rules and which may hold surprises both pleasant and disagreeable.

A second element of pilgrimage is that of community. This may not be immediately apparent to those for whom the classic pilgrim imagery is drawn from John Bunyan's *Pilgrim's Progress:* the individual Christian persisting through the wilderness of this world, the Slough of Despond, Vanity Fair, Doubting Castle, carrying "marks and scars" which ultimately attest "that I have fought his battles who now will be my rewarder". In her closing sermon at Santiago WCC officer Nélida Ritchie, of the Evangelical Methodist Church of Argentina, spoke of another model, that of a group of pilgrims on the way together, coming to learn of "our difficulties in matching our step to the pace of our brother and sister".

The message from Santiago gives thanks for "great strides forward" and asks about the next "steps" God is leading the churches to take. The pace at which these steps will be taken is of course a key question. How can the churches do justice to the urgency of the call towards fuller koinonia while respecting the different speeds at which ecumenical pilgrims move? (As Scottish Reformed theologian Elizabeth Templeton hinted, "professional ecumenists", ever sensitive to such differences, may be "temperamentally disposed to *overestimate* the patience of God".)

Finally, pilgrimage is a spiritual exercise — for ecumenical pilgrims just as much as for the footsore seekers of pardon and grace at the Cathedral of St James. Yet apart from periods of worship, this calling to a deeper spirituality may recede from view in ecumenical meetings. The precise and careful negotiating of agreements and drafting of texts may overshadow the awesome reality that the ecumenical exercise is rooted in what Faith and Order Commission moderator Mary Tanner called "the absolute Christian obligation to show forth the possibility God has for all humanity and for the creation".

In his address in Santiago South African archbishop Desmond Tutu was eloquent in linking the churches' movement towards fuller koinonia with the development of their spiritual resources. Churches, he said, must become "powerhouses of prayer, where vigils and fasts are normal, matter-of-course occurrences. We should grow in holiness and in stillness and contemplation, for we are exhorted, 'Be still and know that I am God'. As we grow closer to God, so we will draw closer — or, rather, we will be drawn closer — to one another."

October 1993

167

VISIBLE HOLINESS

I was not included among the "representative sample of adults" who were contacted by the Gallup organization in July for its annual survey on how people in the United States perceive the "honesty and ethical standards" of various professions, though I was in the US at the time.

This comes as no surprise. Of the vast number of polls that are taken each week to quantify "public opinion" on just about every imaginable subject, none has ever included me.

Perhaps this is just as well. With few exceptions, I suspect I would want to argue with the questions rather than answer them. That would probably mean being classified under *"No opinion"*, *"Don't know"* or *"Uncertain"*, which would scarcely seem to do justice to my reluctance to respond in a way that fits the polltaker's categories.

Even with increased frequency, sophistication and speed of disseminating results, the contribution which opinion surveys make to public discourse seems to me to be at best an ambiguous one; and I have yet to be persuaded that the instant electronic referendums predicted by enthusiastic futurists will represent a giant leap forward for democracy.

Despite these reservations, I read with fascination a recent news release summarizing the results of the Gallup survey on honesty and ethics, headlined "Confidence in Clergy at All-Time Low".

The survey disclosed that just over half of US residents consider clergy to have "high" or "very high" ethical standards. That ranks them fourth — behind (1) pharmacists, (2) university professors and (3) engineers. Though still well ahead of politicians, stockbrokers, sellers of automobiles and television talk-show hosts, their position is dropping. In 1985 two-thirds of the respondents gave the clergy "high" or "very high" ratings, and until 1988 they topped the list of professions.

One might hope that the lower rating reflects a growing theological understanding that while ordination sets specially prepared people aside for particular service in the church, it does not magically exempt them from weakness, temptation and sin. But the news release offered more immediate and probably more likely reasons: recent media coverage of the activities of cults, scandals involving prominent clergy and a general decline, documented by earlier surveys, of confidence in "organized religion".

In mitigation of what seems to be one more piece of bad news for the church, it might be said that when you are in spiritual need, what counts is not the perceived or actual ethical standards of "the clergy" as a whole, but the personal qualities and service of the individual minister to whom you turn. Moreover, the recognition that God's grace can shine through the ministry of even poorly motivated, weak and sinful persons goes back at least to the Apostle Paul.

Indeed. But the combination of a decline in confidence in "organized religion" (however much we may dislike the term) and scepticism about the ethical standards of its full-time employees is a reminder of the insight behind the ecumenical movement that the invisible unity of the church should be reflected in visible unity.

It is an insight that appears in the words that follow "that they may all be one" in Jesus' prayer for his disciples — not only the invisible unity of "as you, Father, are in me and I am in you", but also visible unity, "that the world may believe". Just as striving for the visible unity of the church is essential to carrying out its mission in the world, so we cannot rest easy when the visible holiness of the church seems to be eroding — even if we can explain it, even if we are tempted secretly to relish the scandals that have brought down those whose theology and politics we dislike.

November 1993

DEFINING ISSUES

It was fitting for the Programme to Combat Racism (PCR) to mark its 25th anniversary during the meeting of the WCC central committee in South Africa in January, for PCR and South Africa have always been closely identified.

Over the past quarter-century, PCR has devoted about half its resources and energies to the effort to eradicate entrenched racism in South Africa and neighbouring countries where white minorities legally excluded blacks from the political process. At the same time, many South Africans knew nothing of the WCC except PCR (seen by some as a beacon of hope, by others as the incarnation of the threat of godless communism).

"For years we were banned from this country because of our commitment to combat racism and the sin of apartheid," said WCC president Vinton Anderson during the central committee session marking the PCR anniversary. "And here we are!"

But the celebration was muted. Its tone was gratitude and renewed commitment, not self-congratulatory triumphalism. The combat against racism is far from over. Dramatic changes in South Africa have inevitably turned ecumenical attention to other forms of racism elsewhere. Meanwhile, in South Africa itself, apartheid may be dead, but racism lives on.

In 25 years the Programme to Combat Racism has done much to make the incompatibility of racism with the gospel of Jesus Christ a defining issue for the ecumenical movement — an issue that cannot be left off the agenda because it marks out with such force and eloquence the essence of what the movement is all about.

Enthusiasts, sceptics and opponents alike have seen PCR as a kind of model for thwarting those who would like to sweep critical but divisive topics under the carpet. Indeed, people who feel the WCC is giving their own priorities insufficient attention are sometimes heard to propose that the Council establish similar programmes — to combat sin or unbelief or fundamentalism or substance abuse or militant Islam.

Looking ahead, some observers have suggested other potentially defining issues for the WCC and ecumenical movement.

In his report, WCC general secretary Konrad Raiser noted that violence against women "constitutes a fundamental ethical and social challenge that could well be compared to the challenge of racism and its impact on the ecumenical movement in the 1970s". The very name of the proposed WCC programme to overcome violence suggests explicit parallels with PCR. Others would identify human sexuality as an issue whose potential for dividing churches is at least as great as the controversial PCR grants to liberation movements in Southern Africa.

It remains to be seen whether or not these, like the struggle against racism, become "defining issues" for the ecumenical movement in the years ahead, for defining issues emerge by a process rather more complicated than bureaucratic decisions by governing bodies.

But no matter what shape these and other issues (as, for example, the relation between the gospel and cultures) take on the agenda of the WCC, what is ecumenically significant — and challenging — is that they arise in the context of the commitment to making real and visible the koinonia that is God's gift and calling.

March 1994